Marriage or Mating?

Rules to a Marriage No One Told You

Zahra Akberali

Table of Contents

Dedication

I would like to dedicate the book to people who are less fortunate and especially to those who live their life out of fear, constantly worrying about how the world would judge them.

Acknowledgements

Sofia Larson, Leyla Simbizi, Merline Macaulay & all those who never walked out of my life and believed in me. I have many people to thank, and I want my family and friends to know how much I appreciate their support. I want to thank you all for raising and such a strong independent woman out of me. I am proud of the person I am today, and I am proud to say I am the daughter of my two lovely parents. This book is a dedication to my parents since no matter how much difficulty I experienced while growing up and throughout my childhood, I am here because of those challenges and hardships I have overcome with my parents by my side.

About the Author

Zahra Akberali is a Tanzanian girl from a middle-class family who got married after being madly in love with a husband… A husband who realised he didn't love her anymore. She lives in the UK now, and knowing full well she doesn't have a family here, she yet managed to get a job. It didn't come easy, and she had to face plenty of rejections, but they eventually came to an end. Zahra started from a job at the retail store to an amazing company she currently works at (she's not sure what the future holds, but she's not interested in predicting it). ☺

Becoming a British Citizen was not easy for her – considering she had a tough marriage – especially finance-wise. Despite all the other responsibilities she had, Zahra accomplished getting her British citizenship on her own.

Zahra got independent from a young age, from where she has been supporting her family in spite of all her own personal challenges. She has continued to ensure the survival of her family back in Tanzania and is grateful to God for the strength he always gave her.

After having to go through a difficult life and facing all sorts of challenges (such as sleeping in a basement), Zahra is here today, with the grace of God, renting her own apartment. People desire to own a house, own a car, but her dream has been to "OWN MY BOOK" and to be the author of her own life. Here she is, accomplishing this with a wonderful team at Savvy Marketing.

Preface

I have lived enough life to know what it's like when your life changes and when life changes you. Fortunately, I have seen the good, the bad and the ugly. As much as I would like to forget all that, I can't quite do that. Most of the "ugly" I had to deal with came with my marriage that I have now put behind me by stepping out of it.

I was raised and lived in Tanzania. I moved to the UK after I got married. There I had no family and still get amazed at how I built my own circle of positive friends who lifted me up and people who I started making my family. My divorce has already happened, but I went through a lot since this was an unintentional divorce.

Many women from my culture don't look very kindly to the notion of divorce, but I... well, I believe differently. I feel that a loveless marriage should come to an end as soon as possible or at least before it drives one of the two people in the marriage crazy.

Like other women, when divorce first came up in the relationship between my husband and me, for the longest of times, I refused to accept he didn't love me and didn't want to be married to me. I asked myself questions like, did he ever love me? Why wouldn't he try harder for me?

But then, I already knew the answers to such questions. I do believe when a man does love his woman, he would keep her and fight for her tooth and nail. I didn't feel that way since I was easily asked to leave and was never fought for, and this was disappointing because I loved my husband A LOT.

So the bottom line stands men who refuse to understand and respect what love is cannot love anyone. And what is love, you ask? Love is thinking about the other person. Love is unconditional. It lies in being unselfish. Love is sacrificing for another person. Love is truly expressed when you go half the way or sometimes even 75% or 110% to meet the needs of the person in your life.

Most men don't know what love is, I guess. But that could just be my experience of the man I have been married to. I wouldn't know about other men, of course, but I do know how men think and look at the women in their lives. Most men see women as sexual objects than a whole different person. Such a perspective only brings down the woman in the relationship and turns her into a submissive creature who does as her master tells her to. This often happens when the woman *believes* she has to sacrifice without limits or that such behaviour from her end will allow her to avoid any conflicts in her marriage.

I have been through similar circumstances in my marriage to know exactly what that feels like. I learned, quite late in life, that such an attitude doesn't bring peace and harmony to the relationship you're in. It merely deteriorates it further.

This book is for all the women out there who have been through something like this or have been raised to believe by their culture, religion or traditions that they're the ones who have to carry all the weight in their marriage.

If you truly believe that, know that you're wrong. You deserve a partner of equal standing who contributes to your marriage just as much as you do. Who makes as much sacrifice as you do? Who gives you the room you need in life to create and live your own happiness.

I need you to know that you are worth it all!

Chapter 1: Do What Feels Right

"If it doesn't feel right, don't do it. That is the lesson, and that lesson alone will save you a lot of grief."

- Oprah Winfrey

In many cases, living by the norms and principles of society is important. There are many reasons for it, including protecting ourselves and ensuring security. For instance, think about the decision for marriage itself. Family and friends start reminding you when you come of age and when it's time for you to marry.

Sometimes, the decisions we have to make need to be made upon consultation and after taking suggestions from other people. However, it is a truth universally acknowledged that other people don't always understand what is best for you, and sometimes, they don't want what is best for you either.

It is perhaps for this reason that mystics, sages and many wise people of the world have written on and urged for the importance of listening to yourself. The famous Sufi poet Rumi says, "Hear only the voice within." I'm sure he does not simply mean listening to the voices in your head, which can provoke doubt and all sorts of dissonance. Rather, we ought to listen to something more deep-seated, something way down in the soul, the soul which is the seat of self-

1

knowledge and discloses important truths after deep introspection sometimes.

I have found my life bloom when I have made the important decisions of life, keeping myself first and listening to myself alone. You may ask, why is it important to listen to your feelings? Because feelings come from the heart and soul, that is where intuition and enlightenment are seated. No one knows you better than your own soul than your own heart; in other words, your own feelings.

Sometimes, knowledge is not the only motivator for decision-making. It may surprise you, but while I criticise my husband and other men who do not know what love is, the sad part is that I myself never knew what love was either. My misinformed knowledge had come from my own house, where all of our misinformed knowledge initially comes from. The family I grew up in had taught me love is you doing things for others always, without expecting anything in return. No one stressed the importance of one of the most important aspects of loving, that what it's like to love yourself.

Self-love is just as important as loving others, but I was never told about it. I had to always be the one who sacrificed for the sake of others because that's what I had known and had learned. If I would have listened to my feelings, I would have been writing a different story. Heck, I may not even be able to write a worth-enough story, which is why I am grateful for my experiences and grateful that *I* decided to pen my story down in this book.

Since I did not know about self-love and had a very limited understanding of love, I lived in conflicts, doubts and with a lack of fulfilment. In hindsight, I remember clearly that mine was a life of shackles. It is no surprise then that along my journey, I did not find anyone who would sacrifice for me or would go out of their way to do anything for me – until at the later stage of my life.

I was living an unfulfilled marriage with my husband, as well as an unhappy life, but I was still holding on to it tightly, like someone holding on to thick ropes. My hands were bruising, but I could not care as long as my home was intact, and the society was satisfied. I was eager to be the one who loves and endures, and sacrifices for the sake of others. But I was wrong in many ways. I should have considered what is it that I want.

When my husband eventually urged me to leave him, that's when I got to asking some of the most important questions from myself. These were as follows:

1. If my husband continues the way he does today, do I want to stay married to him?

2. I don't have anything other than what happens today. We are not promised tomorrow. Why don't I use the evidence of what is there before me today and make a decision for myself?

3. We cannot hope for a change that may never come. Why am I holding on to the hope of things getting better tomorrow then if all I have is today?

4. I guess if my husband changed and became the person I hoped for him to become. So why don't I leave him? I can always re-marry him, can't I? (But I knew this would have never been the case).

I was always hesitant for making a decision for myself because in my family, in my community and with all the dictates of morals that existed in our lives, I truly always believed that divorce is a failure. Again, what I knew trumped over what I felt deep inside me, but I could pay heed to it. Most women don't. They take pride in not divorcing, and we force God and our prayers to play along with these morals. But God is not judging us; no figure comes from way up in the clouds and raises a finger at us. The truth is we only judge ourselves in this lifetime. Hence, we should decide according to our judgments and feelings.

I have told you that I had a very difficult childhood growing up. We are all naïve, vulnerable and gullible as children. Others may exploit us, and worse, abuse us, but we never get to understand what's going wrong. However, deep down, we know that something wrong is happening to us, but it gets very hard to recognise abuse. There are all sorts of gas-lighting behaviour, threats and whatnot that restrict us and keep us in fear.

More so, an abuser never admits they are abusing, nor the one getting abuse realises they are being abused. I tried not to be naïve and believe that everyone tells the truth, but that is never the case. As the famous Dr House said, "Everybody lies." Most of the people around you are used to lying; they may not even notice it. The worst kind of lying is lying to oneself, which is also something that people do if it will give them an advantage at all.

I had to tell myself a lot of lies when I believed I had to ensure the persistence of my marriage. But eventually, the veil got off my eyes. I understood that I had to acknowledge the truth. I had to consider what I am feeling, rather than what I knew – that divorce is bad and I will be a victim of disrepute if I leave my husband. This was the point I got to asking myself more questions.

I asked myself, what do I want? Do I still want to stay in this marriage feeling suffocated and drained? And if so, why would I want that? After asking myself this, I realised how long it had been since I had asked myself about my wants.

In the marriage, with the paradigms of love I grew up with, I never realised the importance of putting myself first. I had always put myself second, but things were changing here.

I don't know how many of you, dear readers, have not asked yourself about your wants and desires. If you have not, I want you to take a pause and question yourself this instantly. ***WHAT DO YOU WANT?***

We forget it so often, but we need to remember that we in charge of our lives. We are at the helm, the driver's seat. Our feelings and our intuition are important and valuable. We must not let *anybody* make us feel otherwise.

In my years of marriage, I have had my husband say to me that he would change. He told me it will get better from the very first day. I want you to tell me truthfully, have you ever had your spouse or anybody else you are committed to telling yourself that same thing, that things will get better, that they will improve, and nothing ever changed? If yes, you are one of the many. I had gotten swayed by the same misconception too.

When I started putting myself first, I realised some significant truths. "What did change since he first started promising that?" I asked myself. "Why have I not been able to accept that he was never going to change, neither ever will? Why did I believe he would change? Was it all that hope and misconceptions about love that I was fed up with? And eventually, I started asking the question that led me to write this book for you all: "Why would any women settle for anything less in their life?"

It felt so good. I felt that I could see the matrix. Everything was becoming clear for me. I was being enlightened by my intuition and my feelings and was realising that I had settled for lesser than what I deserved. All my fears were going away, and I was ready to make the big decision. And here we literally are today. So let me ask you, are you ready to make the big decision in your life?

Of course, I cannot simply expect you to understand everything within a matter of a few thousand words. This is not a game or hypnotising session where I snap my fingers, and you wake up to the truth before you. Important truths take their time to dawn on you. You have to therefore take your time with the realisations that may or may not be entering your mind. If the latter is the case, give it some time. We have ten chapters to get over, of course.

Many of you may be stuck in relationships that are terrible, but you just can't see it. In fact, not even relationships, rather many of you may be stuck with dilemmas regarding whether you should make such a decision for your children or even whether your job or your college is taking too much of a toll on you, which you should leave.

I want you to allow the real and suppressed questions to emerge. I want you to take a stand for yourself. At least start with merely entertaining what would a life based on your principles and your rules, and what your feelings look like. Don't just stop here. Imagine it. It's quite beautiful, isn't it? Not having to be reduced and mistreated, having the independence and living and wearing how you want to live and wear. These are important lifestyle decisions, and I want you to think for yourself.

After entertaining similar thoughts, how do you feel? Do you feel free just by imagining a life like this? And then does that feeling of freedom follows a bunch of fears? *What will people think? My family and my husband will disapprove, so I cannot do it.* If these are your thoughts, counter them. Tell yourself that you are important, that your safety, comfort, and especially your happiness is important. Don't let your fears empower your feelings. Choose for yourself, and choose yourself. Do what feels right to you. And that feeling of rightness cannot come at the price of your suffocation.

If you are still confused, let us try something else. A certain indication for what the future of a relationship looks like is looking at how it has been in the past. How has your relationship been with my spouse in the past? Do I have the courage to accept the truth about myself? Can I pronounce that truth out to others who need to hear it? The things that I went through have limited my understanding of things and filled me with biases?

When we really consider it, we realise that choosing for ourselves is not as scary as we think it is. Yes, there may be stepping stones in the way and hurdles, but the end result is heavenly: freedom. You know, I wanted and hoped to have the support of my family and my community in my decision to divorce my husband. Did you think I got it? No, because such a path – i.e. of deciding what feels right – is never easy. Like me, rather than gaining support, you may also get told "compromise to your way of living."

But really, why should anyone compromise with anything that is clearly unhealthy, mentally, emotionally and physically. I am not saying that you should end your relationships at the slightest inconvenience. For some things, it is okay, rather is encouraged to adjust in relationships. Of course, we are humans. We are bound to make mistakes and possess traits that may be problematic for our partners. But what we should not compromise on is when it comes to real problems such as abuse or general unhappiness of relationships.

Thinking back, I wish I had made different choices and did what I felt was right on so many occasions. But I also believe I needed the lived experience to teach me the truth. I felt really abandoned in my relationship and continued to let myself down. It was not my inner wisdom rather my fears and anxieties that went on to set my priorities for me. For what it was worth, I did keep praying to know what is it that I wanted. Eventually, I was led to the right place.

The final questions I had to deal with were as follows. As you read them, also reflect on how these may apply to you:

1. Did I want to continue living in a marriage in which I was not feeling happy?

2. Should I save myself and be the inspiration I can potentially be to those women who feel there is no hope? I can choose to be an example which represents that nobody should tolerate any abuse nor compromise their own happiness to keep the society pleased and satisfied, even though I myself may burn.

And so I made the big decision, with my conscience intact and my heart smiling. I did what I felt was right, and the rush of happiness I felt then is indescribable. So my question to you is, will you do what is right for you?

Conclusion

This chapter dove into the concept of how important it is for us to do what we feel is right. The points of reference and understanding of things we have throughout our lives may have come from misinformed places; it is very important to recognise that. Sometimes, it is important to choose the truth that comes from a place of self-love instead of that other incomplete knowledge others have filled you with. Question yourself. Ask yourself about your wants and desires and the things that will make you happen. That is what I urged you for, and I will continue urging for every chance I get in this book. Instead of listening to other people's advice and doing what others feel is right, which covers us in many fears and anxieties, we ought to choose our happiness and do what we feel is right.

Chapter 2: Always Be Happy & Grateful

I sometimes wonder strongly about the question of happiness in marriage. Do you ever wonder what happiness in marriage is? One can easily say that happiness varies for each individual in a marriage, but still, there have to be some converging points.

Yet, before thinking about happiness or gratitude, one needs to revise what a married couple and married life is. No, I will not have you believe that that fairy-tale notion of two perfect people together living a fantastic life of 'happy ever after'. Sorry to pop your bubble, but that kind of married life is not possible in at least this lifetime.

In a marriage, you both are two imperfect people legally bound together in a communal bond who have vowed to spend their entire lives with each other. In such a communion, shit is bound to happen if I may be so informal. You both will disagree on things. You will fight, hurt each other emotionally and physically, too, perhaps, but you both will get moments where you are happy with each other and are grateful for each other. Hence, the first impulse should be not to quit that marriage if those 'happy' and 'grateful' moments outweigh the sadness and fights.

But now to convey to you the secret about happiness and gratitude in marriage. I have come to this conclusion after having lived an unhappy married life and after observing other happy couples. I now, therefore, know that certain marriages are happy and filled with gratitude because both the members are each other's best friends first.

I've found so many people who think marriage is all sparkles and unconditional love. Nonsense. If I had a dime for every time I heard someone say, "Well, I just don't get that spark anymore, so we broke up..." That is just not realistic. The fact is, love *IS* friendship. You don't put the strain of constantly carrying that spark on a friend, do you? No, you have moments where you sit together in silence and even sometimes don't know how to comfort the friend. But other times, you have a rowdy day filled with risk and adventure. Then the very next day, you are content with a dull day too. All of that goes beyond the 'spark'. What that 'spark' is, it's actually something called 'Limerence'. You can look it up. Limerence tends to die after a year or two, and it is after that that the cloud of friendship settles in.

Imagine that you are married and are able to say: "I have a life partner and a best friend who is committed to me, and I am committed to him in decent synchronicity. He's someone with whom I enjoy hanging out and goofing around, but also being serious, and just overall spending time, no matter what we're doing. He makes me feel that I can be myself around him in a way that I never could with

13

anyone else. Even if I try with others, I will not get that kind of friendly chemistry. It's not like a spark. I don't always get butterflies in my stomach when he touches me or comes near me. But I tell you, we do respect and cherish each other. I love our inside jokes and the little habits/routines that we have. For example, when we're sleeping deep into the night, he would snore every now and then. I would simply make sure to put in my earplugs.

"We enjoy doing several things together, but sometimes it can be mundane too. We also respect each other's right to enjoy our own hobbies or interests that the other person does not relate to. I can be watching TV shows at the same hour while my spouse prepares for their office presentation. Clinginess is not a vital factor in marriage. I can even be in the same room as him and be doing different activities… Yet, in a happy marriage, that still feels as though we are spending time together. I can spend hours without speaking to him, but understand with just a glance that everything is fine between us, that neither person is ignoring the other, but is just indulged in their own different deals. We support each other. We discuss things and communicate when need be, and make sure that we don't attack each other's self-respect. We have disagreements too, but we talk through them or agree to disagree."

Now you know that is not a dreamy kind of married life, that it is practical and possible, so you also know that this is the kind of love that makes you happy and feel gratitude. Like many of the marriages around, I was deprived of that too. I did not understand many things, especially not the fact that my husband doesn't treat me like a friend. I don't feel special with him.

I do not mean that I always want to be in that 'honeymoon phase' in a marriage where things are always different, and love is constantly flowing with adorable gestures being exchanged on both ends. See, dates might be built on roses, and fancy dinners for some, but marriages are more about comfortable trips to the museum, staying in when the other partner has to go out to watch the baby, playing foosball, reading in the library, making grocery lists, and doing just about any other chore or task that you can think of... *together*.

Happiness should not be what your partner wants you to do to fit his convenience. There's a reason why this is a two-way communion. Love and mutual respect are required in this connection. Submissiveness and compromise are not the striking features of marriage. Yes, you both can work on yourself to become better persons. By extension, always be able to work on your marriage when you notice an unhappy pattern.

But this must not lead to endless discussions based on why everything is your fault or their fault. Any real man who genuinely loves you should always say, "I know things are not working out the way we had planned, and I want to work on it. I want us both to feel happier in our marriage. Instead, other spouses and I have gotten told and still get told that *'you'* would have to try harder and harder. That's not fair!

The ideal scenario is that you must expect your spouse to treat you well and mutually then treat your spouse well too. Marriage, in no way, allows your spouse to walk on you or vice versa. If he/she does it, call them out on it. Don't play the victim, nor suppress your hardships either. Don't say, "You always do [XYZ]" card. Instead, say something like, "That was rude. You don't treat your co-workers or long-time college buddies that way, do you? Much less you should treat me that way." Confrontations about disturbing behaviour can be made in a way that the person does not feel disrespected, even if the spouse may have disrespected you in the first place. You both are two imperfect people. You will have to sort your issues out in an organic way. Sometimes people get a little too lax around each other, and that can cause hurt feelings. People need to respect one another: even married people, especially married people.

While I am saying all of this, I was not successful in achieving that mutual respect. I was perhaps failing myself in the process. I kept defending my toxic marriage, and I kept reasoning with my husband because most women do this. The sad thing about our society is that when the victim of a toxic relationship talks about his/her feelings, their sadness is often considered as desperation. We often forget our self-worth in this process. We choose to keep our happiness second, and that's what I was doing. My self-respect was zilch in that bond. I have always been told that God is here to give us the inner peace and wisdom to show us to love ourselves. It is often our very spouse who blocks that godly peace and wisdom. But am I to be blamed for that if it is the general case for a woman to not find her self-worth satisfied?

I often wonder that no man is entirely a bad person, but some bad be bad in some respects, which is enough to spoil your broth. My limits were pushed emotionally and in all the other ways, restricting my happiness and freedom did not make him a good person in my eyes. Men, in general, are not to be blamed for that – my dad was a gem of a person. But some men just don't value and appreciate their marriage enough. They don't give love to their wife and support them if they choose to be ambitious.

This is why I have discovered that one must marry a spouse who is responsible. I honestly cannot stress this enough. If you marry someone who cannot keep themselves from abusing you, spending money, or throwing their dirty laundry all around the house when he returns from work, your life will be ruined. If they cannot keep themselves from drinking, you will end up with a drunk. They don't have to be obligated to work, but they should be roughly as educated as you are if you are to coexist with someone on the same frequency as you. All in all, your spouse should be a developed adult. You need to marry a developed adult.

Responsibility also has to do with realising that you must not abuse your partner. No matter how rich your husband is, he will not be a developed adult if he raises his hand on you. When often anyone experiences abuse of any kind, you can automatically assume they are not in a happy bond. Since that person will only hear words that bring them no joy, no peace and no truth, even if comfort or apology comes, it will often be that such toxic behaviour is repeated because abusers are just only words with no action.

It is very frustrating to be with a person who only speaks words but backs them with no action. Such a person adds no value to your life. For them, it is never about keeping the partner happy but always about fitting in according to what suits them and according to their convenience.

For instance, it's totally possible that you are someone who scatters their laundry around the house. For instance, you can be someone who throws your socks on the floor… then marry someone who also throws their socks on the floor. Then finally, hire a maid or encourage each other to pick up the socks each day, mutually. If you marry an OCD neat-freak while you are a bomb of mess, the marital relationship will explode in your face. If you hate onions and spices, don't marry an Indian chef. If you are a movie fanatic, don't marry someone who believes books are the centre of the universe (and better alternatives than movies).

See, that limerence thing I talked about... it blinds people. You hinge so much on that spark you both have that you are unable to be decently smart to notice the clear red flags. You can be someone who likes public display of affection while your partner only prefers private... A compromise can surely be made on this accord, but you need to bring this to the table. You need to acknowledge that this thing will be something you will have to compromise throughout your life.

All these things that I'm relating to you are the things that keep marriages happy. If you are in a marriage where when something happens in a public scenario, you both glance at each other and just know within what the other person is thinking. That is a happy marriage. And you know what the thing is that sustains a happy marriage? Gratitude.

Where there will be a happy marriage, gratitude will follow. If there is no gratitude, God will block your happiness since you don't treasure it.

Often, you will receive no explicit gratitude from your partner at all, but that's okay. Sometimes, the expression is present in their gaze and the way they hold your hand and when your partner confides in you about a difficult secret. You know you're worth it in that scenario; your spouse makes you feel that.

Often in my marriage, I was called 'Bitch'. In such a situation, there will be no happiness, in fact, there'd be onslaughts of depression and feeling of suffocation. In that scenario, gratitude can never be present. Marriage is not about using toxic words. I had to work so hard to keep my marriage going to reach our goals. I tried, I swear I tried, but I was getting to my worst because my partner was had a different perspective. I cannot emphasise how necessary it is to have a cooperative and collaborative partner. I was therefore deprived and willingly denial of what I deserved as my own right.

I want you to ask yourself, no matter whether you're married yet or not, What is the life that you want? If you ask that before your marriage, then make sure that your spouse's vision syncs with yours. If you're already in a difficult marriage, ask yourself that do you want to believe this toxic person is going to change for good and acknowledge his mistreatment?

One of the issues that came in my marriage was because we lived in my husband's parents' house. I wanted to change that place so that I had a roof of my own. But I always knew deep down that my husband never wanted to leave his parents' house. The convenience of his parents made him too comfortable over his marriage and responsibilities. I continued living like that, but should I have? Would you want you to continue living like that?

From where you are sitting, it may be very easy to realise that my marriage is flawed and unhappy. But when you're in that place, it's like being suspended in space. You don't know which way is up and which down. It is when you zoom out and consider your case from a third person's perspective that you understand things more clearly.

I want you to know that you have choices. What kind of a man you marry or continue your life with, it's a choice that you are entitled to, no matter what another would say. There are always choices to make in real life, and it's best when such choices come from a place of self-love. It is self-love that guarantees happiness in the first place since we are then able to choose partners that will match that level of love we give ourselves and can then give to the partner.

Putting our loved one's happiness first over our own happiness is not the ideal solution or ideal way of carrying a marriage. This may be due to how we may have learned to

21

constantly put our happiness third, fourth, fifth, depending on what the situation is and how many people we are involved with. Such feelings are very normal in years of not knowing what self-love is.

Conclusion

We have seen in this chapter that love is not fantastical. No one is perfect and will not love us fully. To love immortally is not a possibility for a woman or a man. The best way for both partners to be happy and live in gratitude is by treating one another as each other's best friends. Toxic relationships where the self-love and self-respect of a partner are not valued is not true love nor friendship.

At the same time, love is not sacrifice, nor is it compromising your own happiness. Love is definitely not abuse. Marriage is a joyful bond that is a friendly experience of togetherness. Adult love with normal boundaries is sound with healthy compromise (not just compromise).

Flaws and faults may exist in a marital relationship, but the need to work on the relationship should be what dominates in that scenario. Both partners should know well what this means. No one partner can be working on this process on their own, surely. Support has to come.

A relationship is not about limitations, rather it is about courage. That's what it takes to make things work. As Imam

Ali (a.s) says, "Anything that brings you sadness and sorrow in life, you need to walk away from it immediately. It is never worth your time and effort in life."

God never forces us to give up our health and happiness for someone else's convenience and ignorance. If you do that, you will just be like how I was: I felt tired, exhausted and despondent. All that I had imagined for my dreams, my goals, were unrealistic. You will feel betrayed and used, and nobody will be blamed but you.

You will feel zero at the end of the day because you have not in the first place valued your happiness. I have faced the same experiences as many of you may be facing. All those sleepless nights, those bruises, those cuts on my body, even getting to a point where I didn't even have a roof over me. No money, experiencing depression, those tears of blood and thoughts of being a failure (which I was not and you are not). How can you come out of this with happiness and gratitude?

Therefore, choose yourself, choose your happiness that comes from that place of self-love, and you will be gratified.

Chapter 3: Stay Around People Who Believe In You

Sometimes we all need someone who believes in us just a little bit more than we do ourselves in order for us to become stronger.

-Raphael Love

Have you ever seen a child - happy and carefree? Have you noticed the ballads in a kid's giggles, how pure and innocent they are? They show that the child has no worries. The only pain a child would feel is of the wounds of broken bones after falling on the rough surface of the ground, that too after playing. Do you ever realise how pure a child's heart is? It's clear as crystal!

Have you ever tried listening to children's plans? When they talk or make decisions amongst themselves, they come up with some of the craziest ideas, but all they do is quite harmless.

Children never envy, hate, take revenge or harm anyone. This is what makes them innocent. Do you know why they are so happy? Nothing is impossible for them. They always believe in themselves and others. They don't time trusting people. That's the reason we often have to tell children to stay away from strangers because they trust too quickly.

Children always think they are surrounded by people who love them.

Kids even see the positive, brighter side of the stories they hear from their elders. They often create scenarios in their little minds through strong imaginations. Their fascination is the world they live in, which makes them happy and cheerful, and they never expect anything in return.

I always wondered what makes them different from adults, and then I understood it's the expectations or rather lack of expectations that keep them happy and content in their lives.

Children don't 'expect' anything from anyone, and they 'trust' everyone.

The same children turn into us when they grow up. As we grow up, we face many adversities and differences all around us. All of this steals our essence and charm. We forget what it's like being a kid. We put so many layers on our personalities, the purest and the finest part of us, our soul – *the child,* is lost somewhere.

The key is to keep your inner child 'alive', no matter what happens in your life and how cruel life becomes for you. You must ask yourself:

What will you do in your power and ability to not let that small child inside you suffer from fear and anxiety?

How you shape your weaknesses, fear, anxiety, uncertainty and worry depends on your willpower, and this depends on your inner child and how you help this child connect with the people in your surroundings.

You meet a lot of strangers in life, each carrying a unique set of personalities and a different vibe from the other. You must have noticed, you feel happy and bright in the presence of some people but burdened and gloomy with certain people around you. The kinds of people you meet, sit with and talk to play a vital role in your overall personality. You absorb others' energies, and you send yours to them. This is the law of attraction. It comprises your upbringing, surroundings and personal traits.

"You are the average of the five people you spend the most time with."

-Jim Rohn

I have a strong belief that an individual whose preferences and tendencies are not the same as ours cannot give us the pleasure we anticipate from them. So, we look for people who resemble us in heart and soul. If you're good, you need good people with you. Toxic people will just make your life more difficult.

The more time we spend with good people, who always strive to bring the best out of us, who always value us, who cherish our presence and wish for our well-being, the more positive and happier we will feel. On the other hand, if the people around us are pessimists, who always complain, highlight our shortcomings and see the glass 'half-emptied' instead of 'half-filled', we will automatically feel the way they do.

Imagine only having negative energies around you. You will not see any spark of happiness in your life. There will only be the dark side in front of your eyes. If we blend in with the awful people, we will get their negative behaviour patterns and feel awful ourselves. Likewise, if we blend in with a positive gathering, it will honour us as well. Our character would be moulded into one held by our friends. That is why it is a true saying that *a man is known by the company he keeps*. Trust this. You should stay around people who make you see the world from a different perspective.

Have you ever asked yourself what happiness is for you? What is the one thing that makes you genuinely happy despite your sufferings? The most important thing you need to assess is the kind of people you are spending most of your time with. You need to check the joy you feel being with them, the value-addition they bring to your life and the level of motivation they provide to bring the best out of you.

Besides, you should start taking steps to change your situation and find happiness. Slowly and gradually, improve yourself to be a better version of yourself every day, the one you would be proud of in times to come.

Love Yourself

The first step to finding happiness is loving yourself. When you love yourself, only then you are able to spread love to people and share happiness. You learn to respect yourself, and you understand there is a purpose for your existence. No one stays with you forever but yourself. All you need is *YOU!* Do more things that make you happy, and do them more often. Keep reminding yourself. You are good enough. You have all the capabilities to achieve everything in the world and hence, build self-confidence within yourself.

"Loving yourself starts with liking yourself, which starts with respecting yourself, which starts with thinking of yourself in positive ways."

– Jerry Corsten

You should not expect anyone to treat you in a certain manner. Rather, surprise yourself with a good movie, a hangout to a serene place, a lunch or a dinner date, a pleasing attire – whatever you might expect to do for someone you love, do it for yourself.

We are often mistreated by others because we expect them to treat us the way we treat them – with goodness, kindness, empathy and loyalty, but when these expectations aren't met, we are disheartened. We should never expect anything from anyone. Walk away from people, who can't see any good in you, who make you feel less valued, less important, and add no value to your life. Your energy is important. Do not waste it on people who take you for granted, who only remember you as per their moods and wishes. Be surrounded by people who are selfless and who genuinely care for you.

"Always strive to become a better version of yourself. The only person whose approval you need to seek is your own. Bitterness and anger will only hinder your happiness."

- Angelique R. Menks

Do Not Feel Ashamed of Anything at Any Cost

Life is a collection of many moments: happy, sad, loud and silent. We go through struggles that are not appreciated by society. Do you ever realise how status-conscious society becomes sometimes? It needs fancy outcomes even in the most miserable situations. The dilemma is, it always wants us to show the glittery side of what we go through, no matter how breaking the circumstances are for us, society only wants what is 'respectable' in its eyes, but we need to learn that life is not equal for everyone.

"Never be ashamed of yourself. Be proud of who you are, and don't worry about how others see you".

-Kristen Butler

Life is a complete process from birth till death. We grow our expectations, dreams, efforts, failures, struggles, tears and joys to become what we want. There are hard times. We often feel we are stuck at one point, and we can't move forward from here onwards, but the only thing that keeps going is LIFE. It never ceases for anyone. It never takes any break.

While climbing up the ladder of life and continuously striving to achieve our goals, there comes a time when we fail miserably, we fall down, and the world makes fun of us. But we should never be ashamed of our failures. We should not be shy about our struggles. We should learn from them and keep the lessons they teach in our minds. We should never be afraid of starting over from scratch. Whatever comes our way, we must go through it in order to grow through it.

Do Not Make All the Changes at Once

When you start loving yourself, you take the next step to move forward and bring improvements in your lifestyle, mindset, your goals and ambitions. Do you often think there is a lot going on in your mind? There's so much on your plate, and you want to get everything done in no time. Relax! Remember, it is not necessary to start big to succeed in life. Consistency is the key. In order to achieve big, you have to begin with baby steps, one at a time. No matter how big the goal is or how unachievable it seems, it is always possible. You should break it into small, attainable steps that you think are possible for you. Make little investments every day and give your best. Focus on quality over quantity. No doubt you will have confusions, fears and uncertainties, but only you can become a better version of yourself through repetitive work on yourself and your goals every day.

"You don't have to see the whole staircase, just take the first step."

-Martin Luther King Jr.

Let's say you want to make a career progression and become an entrepreneur, or buy a big house, or love a brand

31

new Lamborghini, but right now, you have no plan on your table. You should jot down the 'most important' and 'most urgent' tasks to achieve first. Make short-term goals, work on them, achieve them, track your progress and find the grounds that require improvement. Once you are fully satisfied with your achievements, increase the horizon, make long-term goals and plan accordingly. You have to nurture your idea and wait patiently till it becomes mature enough, and then you can move your attention to a new venture.

Just as we do for a good recipe, we do not put all ingredients into the pot at once. You should not try to change everything in your life at the same time. Change is inevitable. It will eventually occur. What matters the most is how you prioritise your life.

"The key is not to prioritise what's on your schedule, but to schedule your priorities."

-Stephen Covey

Be Smart and Brave

To move on in life, you have to be neutral. You have to make smart moves without letting anyone down or without hurting others. You must be brave enough to accept yourself first, for who you are, what your strengths and weaknesses are, and how you can overcome your fears with your strengths. Learn to be real, to accept things for how they are. There are obstacles in life, and we must pass them gracefully, like a warrior, without giving up. Be brave to learn from your mistakes and turn your weaknesses into your strengths.

Let's face it. We are not robots. We are not controlled through any chemical formulae or remote controls. Rather, we have emotions, we have our sentiments, and we have our moods. We think we plan, and we make things happen to the best of our capabilities. However, once we have taken action, it's out of our hands to mould a certain result or to redirect the plans always in our favour. We face success and failure. We must accept the reality we can only control our own efforts and hard work, but results also depend on luck. If our plans are destined to be successful, we should be happy, but if we fail, we must be grateful for the lesson we learned through this failure.

Trust Your Guts

We have been rewarded with an instinct. It's a universal fact. So, when you listen to your instincts, it helps you gauge the people, surroundings and situations in a better way. Your judgement plays an important role in the actions you take. In your life, many people have a perception of you. They may have good intentions for you, while some are loyal or fair to you. This is where your 'gut' alerts you – listen to it! Trust it.

At times, there are conflicts in what your gut tells you and what society says about a particular person or situation. You must listen to your intuition in such situations because it doesn't betray. It will save you from making mistakes most of the time.

Have Faith in What You Pray

A prayer is a powerful tool that connects us with our Creator, the Almighty God. It's the trust we put in His hands that whatever we desire will be fulfilled and granted to us. Prayer increases your faith and belief. The Creator is the one who comforts us when we are in distress. Faith and prayers both have the power that can heal any situation you are in. Believe in it, but first, believe in yourself, work hard and then leave everything on Almighty. You must think positively to attract the positive because this is the law of attraction – positive thinking have positive outcomes, and negative thoughts bring negative results. Put all your efforts into a plan and pray for the best to happen, but also be prepared for the worse.

"What you believe, you can achieve."

– Mary Kay Ash

Be Grateful, Always!

If you look around, you will find a plethora of reasons to be happy about, to be grateful for, and to be proud of. Above all, the most important thing is to be grateful for whatever you have been blessed with.

In any and every situation, learn to be grateful for the blessings you have been bestowed upon, for the facilities you are enjoying in life, for being in perfect shape, to have all the senses that make you independent of asking help from others, to be able to work on yourself, to be worthy enough, to be helpful to others. Be grateful to be the chosen one. *You are fortunate!* Life is in these little moments. What you have today will become a memory tomorrow, and then, you will only be able to cherish or regret it. So, why not make the most of what you have today! Cherish the little moments and learn to stay happy in them. Celebrate the people you have in your life, the ones who value you, because tomorrow isn't promised to anyone. You never know who will not be there with you the next moment. Be grateful for life and the little challenges that come with it. Time is not always the same. If you had a bad day today, you would not necessarily have one tomorrow as well. Be grateful for the food you eat because there are so many people who are starving. Be grateful for the tough job you have – there are many who can only wish to have a career.

Live your life to the fullest, create memories, spread love and kindness, so when you look back tomorrow, you will have good memories with you as treasures. Such memories will become a source of serenity and calmness for the-then hard times in your life.

Remember, life never guarantees permanent happiness, neither does it promise sad days only. What you sow today, you will reap tomorrow. Practice to live a joyous life from now onwards, embrace all hardships. Be strong in yourself.

"Whatever life throws at me, I'll take it and be grateful for it as well."

-Tom Felton

The Superheroes of My Life

Throughout my life, my struggles have made me a strong woman. My story reveals this to the readers. Despite this, there were some times when I, too, needed a shoulder to lean on. That's how we humans function, right? We always need a support system for our energies. I am thankful to those three beautiful ladies who have always been there for me.

When I had constrained relations with my parents in my childhood, and later on, there were difficulties in my married life, when I fought with anxiety and deep depression, *this* lady gave me true confidence in myself. I want to thank her from the depth of my heart, for she would be experiencing several other difficult emotions from me, including fear, guilt, anger, sadness, and irritability. The traumatic events I went through had made me numb to realise the fact of how complicated I had become, but she never neglected me and loved me in my worse.

She always believed in me, and I will always be grateful to her for this. In my most crucial times, she did not leave my hand and guided me like a shiny star. No matter how many times I fell, she helped me in standing up on my feet again. She gave me light to see in the darkness.

I want to cheer for another woman who has been very patient with me in my hard times. She was my emotional strength, and her presence was the most considerable support for me at times. She provided a listening ear to me. What a great listener she was! She trusted me when no one did and lifted me with the comfort I needed the most. Thank you!

My third hero of the story is this woman, who aided me in my early days of struggle. When I didn't have any money, no proper house to live in, and dwelling in a basement regardless of the intense weather, she sheltered me. She kept me safe in her home – warm and safe. Not only this, she was selflessly there to support me financially, and I can't thank her enough for this. Through my book, I would like to acknowledge that these women have played a vital role in what I am today. I love you all!

Conclusion

In this chapter, we learned how important it is to have good people around us who play an important role in forming our present. The people who surround us today will shape our future. We decide who stays with us to make us, hold us or break us. Self-love is not selfishness. Love for the world starts with a love for one's own self. We learned how important it is to become self-sufficient, confident and strong for ourselves.

"Life is fragile. We're not guaranteed a tomorrow, so get it everything you've got."

-Tim Cook

Sofia Larson, who truly never left my hand and guided me on my most critical times when especially I had suffered anxiety, depression and loads of scary times she chose to continue supporting and giving me the light from wherever she was. Most importantly, she always believed in me.

Leyla - she was emotionally always there.

Merline Macaulay – she mainly provided me with a home to stay in when I was sleeping in the basement and took care of all my expenses.

Plus with all my other friends/ family I want to thank who continued to support me in one way or the other).

Chapter 4: Know That Life Is Way Too Short for Regrets

Life is too short to wake up with regrets. So love the people who treat you right. Forget about those who don't. Believe everything happens for a reason. If you get a chance, take it. If it changes your life, let it. Nobody said life would be easy, they just promised it would most likely be worth it.

-Harvey MacKay

Life is short. We all hear this repeatedly, but do you ever realise how literal this is? Imagine you have health, wealth which keeps you peaceful mentally, and a life full of adventures, happiness and ambitions with your family, friends and loved ones. You think this is eternal, and nothing is going to change ever. You save money, take care of your health, and your beloved people are always around you. A lucrative life anyone could dream of, with no sadness from the past or worry for the future.

You assume everything will remain the same, but hey, hold on! Suddenly there's a jolt that turns the life upside down. You have a financial downfall, lose a dear one, miss specific profitable growth opportunities that could be good for your future, your trustworthy friends betray you, and everything makes you believe that you have lost happiness.

Do you know why? It is because you had marked the radius of happiness around these myths.

When everything was favourable, you never realised the importance of things and people, but one bounce changed the meaning of eternity for you. You learn the lesson that nothing is permanent, no one stays forever, and you cannot always win on all grounds of life. You opinionate life as unfair, unpredictable and challenging, and it will never change now - although this is just a phase.

Life is not always perfect. Like a road, it has many bends, ups and downs, but that's its beauty.

-Amit Ray

Blessing In Disguise

Now, visualise a life full of hardships and unfavourable events, but you can deal with all this because of the confidence you possess and the consistency and 'belief' in yourself. Things aren't easy, but you never surrender. Still, your decisions are a failure and trials for you. What would you think if this happens repeatedly?

I am sure you will call yourself *'unlucky'*, and this will develop pessimism to think life a burden only, but may I tell you *THIS* is the best time of your life? The ideal time to reflect and self-evaluate, change your perception, and work on your visions in a brand new way. You need to retain the diminished confidence you already have and keep the positivity alive. Everything you think makes an impact on your life – today and tomorrow. When everything is lost, or life seems meaningless, this is the best time to take a risk and unfold the surprise life has for you.

It is during our darkest moments that we must focus to see the light.

-Aristotle

Take Risk or Regret

When life seems complicated, we lose the reason to be happy. Every trial feels over the top, and we fail to contain them. Despite the toughness, life never goes out of our hands. It doesn't end as often as it feels like it does. We can control our thoughts to change the way and direction we have for our life. I firmly believe that it's a matter of little courage to switch negativity into positivity by trying a little harder and take the risk. Otherwise, we will blame ourselves for being indecisive and fearful of bringing a significant change in life. Happiness is the key to a successful life, but failures are the lessons of a lifetime. The great art is to stay happy even if there is no reason to be happy. Successful people learn this with time and make it a habit to accept the results as they are.

If there is no risk, there is no reward.

-Christy Raedeke

The worst thing to have in life is *'Regret'* - a haunt for life. Regret of not making a timely decision (no matter how right or wrong!), not loving the people the way they deserve, holding grudges, missing an opportunity out of unseen fear, and the regret of wasting time. You have to come out of these guilts that should not contain an inch in your heart.

Always do your best. Your best will change from moment to moment; it will be different when you are healthy as opposed to sick. Under any circumstance, do your best, and you will avoid self-judgment, self-abuse and regret.

-Don Miguel Ruiz

Positivity and Happiness

I aim to change the perception you look at your life. Nothing stays forever, bad days shall pass too, and you have to trust this. Do you look around you to inhale the freshness? Aren't there are so many little things that bring a glimpse of *'positivity'*? Do you not see that the sun rises with new hopes, opportunities, and beginnings every day without any expectations? The sun lightens the world with its bright sunshine and spreads the message of positivity. The first ray of the sun touching the earth ends the darkness. We also require such a bright ray to end the gloom of our life.

Be like the *'sun'*, bright, shiny, and selfless. A source to bring light to others life and make them 'hopeful' with warmth. Do you look at the flock of birds, chirping and flying with glee on a wide-spread blue sky, with intermittent white clouds here and there? The birds enjoy the life of THAT moment only, with no fear for tomorrow and no regrets of yesterday. They firmly believe that shelter and food are promised, so why worry! Be like the *'birds'*, free and delightful. Fill your heart with such positivity and trust that you start feeling to flee too. This is how *positivity* does miracles and generates a happy feeling in our hearts.

You're off to great places, today is your day. Your mountain is waiting, so get on your way.

-Dr. Seuss

Deal with the Hardships

I talked about keeping your inner child alive in my previous chapter. Our inner child gives us the soothing shelter when we come under the scorching hardships of real life as adults. Our inner child creates playful fantasies which are always colourful and optimistic. We forget the reality and stay in our imagination as an 'escape' as long as they make us happy. An adult's life is not easy. There are

43

challenges, competitions and a continuous race to become better day by day. The competition never lets us rest.

Like any game, there can be fouls, unfairness and defeat despite all our efforts and capabilities. It will help if you learn to control your actions and reactions in all situations. You may not always win for the world, but you are a winner already with control over yourself. It's a matter of choice, 'Your choice!'

Your strength doesn't come from winning. It comes from struggles and hardship. Everything that you go through prepares you for the next level.

-Germany Kent

The key is to strive to make a difference and keep moving forward. You only live once, and if you move in the right direction, with a positive mind and a smile on your face, you will find beauty in every difficulty.

Be Compassionate

Smile is the best tool to make friends. A natural ingredient to solve problems and to alleviate the agonies of life. Have you ever thought, what makes us 'human'? It's the compassion and empathy we have for others -the ability to experience others' miseries exactly as they feel. To understand someone's pain, to have the magic to wipe off their tears and gift them a smile from yours is priceless. Compassion is the selfless happiness we experience in ourselves. Nothing wins over the feeling of mending a broken heart.

A simple smile. That's the start of opening your heart and being compassionate to others.

-Dalai Lama

I will not limit this to humans only. The purest form of love is when you help the non-humans, who can never return you any favour. Did you ever see a starving cat on the street and fed it with milk or food? Or did you see a helpless, injured bird lying on the ground, which is losing hope to fly on its wings again, and you healed it because you couldn't bear its suffering? What you offer others will eventually come back to you in a multiplied form. If you spread love, you will receive much love. If you cultivate any negative emotion, you will harvest the extended fruit for the same. It would be best if you do not give up, and I promise you will always feel better by giving generously.

Love Begins Within Yourself

Take some moments out of your routine to meditate on your purpose. Close your eyes to visualise your felicitous present and the things you have handy at that moment to give yourself a chance to resonate where you are standing and what blessings you have, which others do not have. After this self-actualisation practice, you will be grateful to the Almighty for everything He has bestowed upon you. This feeling will create endless gratefulness in your heart for everything you took for granted earlier. It's not necessary to always do something and stay occupied. If you don't do a thing one day, it is perfectly alright. Give yourself periodic rests.

If you feel stuck, lose direction, and don't know what to do, don't panic. Often, we fail to prioritise the 'important' and 'urgent' things in our life. We devalue our physical and mental well-being after our routine lives. The only person who can bring variety to your life is *'YOU'*. Do things that make you happy and satisfied inside. Involve in activities that are good for your growth.

I will advise you to give yourself a break occasionally and bring a change in your monotonous life. Go on a vacation to a beautiful place with your favourite people. Spend more time with nature and focus more on your well-being, but commit yourself first that you will not think about anything when you are out to have peace.

Love yourself unconditionally, because if you don't, who else will!? To appreciate others, you first need to enjoy yourself for how far you have come in life. Leave all the toxicity there before coming back to your life. This shall be a fresh start. Don't think much, and if possible, don't think at all - about people, about past, about future. Focus only on the moment you are living in and make sure you are thoroughly enjoying it. If you say 'I am happy', be sure you mean it.

Sometimes small setbacks are just blessings in disguise.
They enhance your determination and whole-hearted
dedication to achieving your goals.

-Robert Cheeke

Importance of Acquaintances

Ideally, friends are essential, but if you cannot find people syncing with your personal or professional goals, you should stay alone and be your friend. It may sound tricky, but not impossible. Be your critic, your own friend and work for your progression.

I told you to be around people who are suitable for your mental health. This lesson is so important, and it shapes all aspects of your life – whether professional or personal. The kind of people you spend your time with play a vital role in your growth. Your family is your first school, where you learn the basics. The fundamental lessons taught by positive minds stays with us all our life. What one believes teaches forward. That's what shapes us.

The friends you have are the stars that would either illuminate you or darken your abilities. Even if you don't find good people, you are independent to achieve your goals with your potential. We are not machines that are programmed in a fixed pattern. We are irrational sometimes, and we do not have any clue if we are stuck in life. It's natural. Being stuck may hinder our progress, but the key is not to give up and keep going.

Learn to enjoy every minute of your life. Be happy now. Don't wait for something outside of yourself to make you happy in the future. Think how precious the time you have to spend, whether at work or with your family. Every minute should be enjoyed and savoured.

-Earl Nightingale

Your Relationship Is What You Make It

People these days are not happy with their relationship because of the differences they have – in personalities, in habits, in perceptions. It is crucial for a happy relationship that we have a clear set of guidelines mutually agreed that keeps a relationship sound and comforting. We must accept each other the way they are instead of changing them into the person we want to see in them. We will only leave our partner's originality, which will lessen the charm and intimacy of this beautiful companionship. We can prevent a relationship failure this way.

Instead of focusing on that circumstances, you cannot change – focus strongly and powerfully on the circumstances you can.

-Joy Page

First, deal with yourself and make your inner self happy. Be sure that you accept yourself the way you are, and if you find something that is not good even for you, work on it. Be open to your companion, share happiness as well as sadness, and never lie. Besides, for a happy relationship, giving space to each other is very important. In the light of my experiences, I will always advise you to be a 'haven' and a confiding soul for your partner. Keep telling them that you love each other and always there for each other no matter what life brings to you. Put your efforts to understand your partners, cherish their achievements, give a helping hand even if not asked, and repeat all this until you feel real happiness.

The regret of my life is that I have not said 'I love you' often enough.

-Yoko Ono

Focus more on blessings than on something you do not have. Refrain your mind from making scenarios and assumptions which do not exist. Nothing is perfect in the world, every challenging moment feels like it will stay forever, but trust me, everything passes with time and teaches us lessons for a better future. No matter what we do with our lives, God is always kind and merciful to us. He never leaves us in despair. He will take us out to light when we lose our path in the dark if we trust Him, and we keep praying to him, as I said earlier. God loves us the most. That's why He tests us sometimes through hard times and through good times, too.

Lighten up on yourself. No one is perfect. Gently accept your humanness.

-Deborah Day

You Become What You Think

Most of our troubles are inside our 'mind', which leads to overthinking, and then we make bad scenarios that are never going to happen, we are overwhelmed with our thoughts and disturb the peace of our mind, and we keep thinking and waste our precious present. On the contrary, sometimes we create fantasies in our minds and keep idealising relationships and glorifying our role like some spotless, heroic saviour. We ignore the flaws in our imagination, and

50

this gives us a sense of accomplishment. For this time being, we forget our problems and realise they don't matter.

Let's do this more often and implement our fantasies in life until they become a reality. What we repeatedly think will eventually train our minds to act in that particular manner.

What seems to us as bitter trials are often blessings in disguise.

-Oscar Wilde

I shared my experiences of difficulties I encountered in life, the problematic marriage I have been in. My experiences made me a strong woman today. It did not make me a hard or harsh person. It made me an empath who knows what pain is. I have seen the bitterness of life, which is why I promised myself to help those who need help with dealing with life hardships. I can't take away the pain, but I may soothe others with my words in the tiniest possible way, that is, by sharing my experiences through my life story. Trust me. This 'care' is the love we spread without doing anything.

I have learnt to love myself after missing this feeling in my life for a long, and I am confident I have abundant love for people who need it the most. I am not justifying my happiness or contentment in life, but I am happy with what I have. I wish to show people that life is much more than the darkness, which often covers its beauty.

Hard times come and go, but what we make others feel during their hard times or what others do for us is something that leaves a watermark forever. Through love, kindness and prayers for others, we can create a better world where we won't regret NOT doing anything for anyone. God loves those who help His mankind. For the love of God, we should spread love and happiness and make this world a better place to live.

Conclusion

In this chapter, we see the brighter side of the world through the author's eyes. We can't control life, but we can control the way how we live it. We have the power to embrace the change, and ultimately we will see a reformed person tomorrow than we were yesterday. We should smile often and give smiles to those who have lost theirs. Our focus should be on the goodness in everything and the positivity everyone has.

We should learn to ignore the flaws of people and love them by heart. Love makes our hearts free from jealousy and negative influences that distract us from focus – the moving ahead. You don't have to look at your back. You are not going that way. We should be lenient to release ourselves from the aches of the past, the regrets of the voids we left behind, and to feel lighter.

Kindness is a language that everyone understands. If we can't do anything for anybody, the least we can do is to be kind to people – through words, actions, and prayers. We can always pray for them to have ease in life.

Keep your face to the sunshine, and you cannot see a shadow.

-Helen Keller

Chapter 5: Never Leave the Key to Your Happiness in Someone Else's Pocket!

"Don't compromise yourself. You're all you've got."

-Janis Joplin

Over the years, I have learned a simple formula. We are the caretaker of our life's matters, happiness, sadness, grief or celebration. We have the power in our hands to control our emotions and use them as the situation demands. We can't make someone responsible for our happiness. This is my experience. Taking care of happiness is a significant responsibility that should be handled with care, and trusting anyone with this will be a risk. Happiness is a precious feeling, and it should not be compromised. We know our choices the best, what we want for pleasure. We know how to deal with our insecurities better than anyone else.

As I said, you have to love yourself unconditionally before you give love to others. You must learn to accept the originality you have, and this is the first step towards love: *self-acceptance.* You must consider yourself as the most important person in the world. The rest comes secondary.

"You are imperfect, permanently and inevitably flawed. And you are beautiful."

-Amy Bloom

My emphasis is that everyone should love the people around them, which include close relations like family, friends and life partners, but this should not stop a person from self-love. There isn't any limit to the love we give or take. Respect is earned, and I admire the idea that we should respect everyone, but I do not think it should divert us from taking care of ourselves. If we are not taking care of ourselves, we don't feel being loved. How would we spread it to others? I will not appreciate doing this to myself, ever. Love is a supreme emotion.

As I mentioned earlier, love starts *within yourself.* Similarly, happiness is an inside job that starts *'in'* your heart. You are the creator of your happiness. Do you think someone is strong enough to guarantee you 'happiness', while you are struggling with your own battles? Of course not. To make someone happy is the hardest thing possible!

"To say 'I love you' one must know first how to say the
'I'."

-Ayn Rand

I had a few people in my life who motivated me every time when I felt down, and they were my source of happiness. Being with them was a joy for me because I trusted them and handed over my happiness' key in their hands. Apart from any materialistic object, certain people can bring joy to you, too.

Yes, there can be multiple factors that bring the frolic feeling in us, but only if we allow them. We have the key in our hand to open the treasures of happiness, and pick our favourite jewel, be it a kind-hearted human as a friend whose company makes us forget the troubles of life, having a deep conversation with an understanding person of similar attributes as ours, a scenic place which is a joy to our eyes, a lovely book that takes us to an imaginary world of positivity, a giggling baby which instantly makes us smile, a purring cat, or a mouth-watering food that satisfies our taste buds. There are infinite sources, you name it, which we are free to bring in for making ourselves happy, then why providing any other person with this huge *'responsibility'*?

"You stop worrying about things, just go with the ones you like, and there you'll find happiness and joy."

-Auliq Ice

In relationships, we often become unconcerned when it comes to checking how our beloved treat us. We live off our happiness and respect in their hands because our love makes us weak and dependent. It happens the other way around too. We often treat the people who love us as a commodity while they are living beings. Love does not accord anyone to disrespect at any point. It must not be an excuse. I do not preach the stance to be obsessed with treating someone as per our moods and willingness. It creates discord and loses the beauty of commitment.

"You can't change how people treat you or what they say about you. All you can do is change how you react to it."

-Mahatma Gandhi

Relationships are fragile. If we do not understand the nature of our partners, there will be no companionship and harmony. Compatibility between the partners is the acceptance of each other's ideologies, philosophies, habits and willingness. We will not be able to give them the love and respect they deserve if there is no acceptance, which goes both ways.

While striving for a better life, there will be failures too. Situations are not favourable every time. The challenges we come across make us vulnerable, sensitive and reactive. They shape us in a way that we forget the essence of happiness. We become bitter, but I have told you from my own experiences that hard times do not last forever. The feeling to be lost should not stay with us for long either. It's okay to fall, but it's not okay to NOT stand up again.

During our weak moments, we incline towards trusting others easily. These are the moments when we think others will bring us back to life and make us happy. In actuality, this never happens. People do not understand our situation well, and hence, their words and actions hurt us instead of mending. Our expectations from people are ruined, and the impression of becoming happy gets blurred. As a result of this, we lose the people who hurt us, but we learn the lesson of NEVER trusting anyone to make us happy. It's not their job. They will never meet our expectations. It's our responsibility. Happiness comes with trust, and we should be the most trustworthy for ourselves.

"To be happy, we must not be too concerned with others."

-Albert Camus

Life is all about challenges and failures, one after another, right? Failing should never be a shame or guilt to stop us from moving forward. Learn to forgive yourself so that you are ready for the other battles. We can't afford to stop at any point for long. The sufferings should not be prolonged, else we will never meet our life goals. Fail, suffer and then heal yourself, but make sure that you do not bring this guilt of failure into your heart again.

The world treats you bitter, and it is already there to test your patience for the things you do. You, at least, must never be too hard on yourself. I have been repeating to stay around such people who lift you, motivate you to do better each day and be the best version of yourself. This is a life lesson I learned, and hence, passing it over to you all as well.

If you can't change your environment and surroundings, change yourself to the extent to tune in with the world. We cannot change the world or the people around us, but we can change the way we look at them. It is not our responsibility to change the whole world at once, however, we can try to adjust in a particular situation.

I told you about the difficulties I faced in my marriage. There were incompatibilities between my husband and me. He never loved me the way I had expected from him. My marriage tested my patience in all possible ways. Despite the difficulties I faced, my husband did not accept that there could be any failure from his side too. He never took any responsibility for this, especially not at the beginning. At the later stage, he did come apologising to me and admitted to wishing that the divorce did not happen. I do believe he said that genuinely out of guilt. He felt bad, and I have forgiven him and myself too, particularly because I had healed. As they say, of course, "forgiveness comes with healing."

But before that realisation, he never cared if being with him made me happy and satisfied in our relationship. People say that marriage is about sacrifice, but not so much for me. It is more about acceptance towards each other and working hard mutually towards the goal you want to reach.

A great obstacle to happiness is to expect too much happiness.

-Bernard Le Bovier

This was my mistake that I 'expected' him to make me happy, love me, and work on the lack of this relation. I trusted him with the key to my happiness, while he was least interested in having me in his life.

We always commit to each other when we enter into a relation called 'marriage'. It's a two-way responsibility and a mutual agreement that we shall be responsible for filling each other with love and care. We will protect the sanity of each other's minds. It is a strong bonding that can't be broken no matter what life throws on us. This was my ideology when I got married. I expected the same from my partner that he would be a source of peace in my life through love and happiness.

"Love is that condition in which the happiness of another person is essential to your own."

-Robert A. Heinlein

When there is no love and the expectations are not met, the relation can't survive for long. The word 'love' has magic and power in itself, but no one can prove it just by saying 'I love you' to someone. Their actions should mean it. The things we do for someone out of love should be self-explanatory, even if we never say it. As they say, *actions speak louder than words*. Whatever we say will be meaningless if we don't act what we say. Love is more about 'showing' than telling.

Do you notice the way people treat you? Do you ever feel how their presence make you feel? The vibes they give you say a lot about the intentions they have in their hearts. If you feel happy around some people, you will trust them automatically. This is natural, and the fact is, people will be more open to those who they trust and like. This trust creates a sense of commitment, an association to cherish their presence.

The reality is, everyone is selfish. People always take care of their benefit, even if it is at the cost of someone else's peace. If you are happy, you should take care of your happiness and not expect others to safeguard it. People punish us for our faults, no matter how tiny they are.

My husband never tried to change himself for the marriage. A real change means growing up, taking care of things and preparing for the best and worst to come. I didn't see my husband growing up to the level to take care of his things. You see, if the person doesn't take care of himself and not mature enough to understand what's good or bad, he would not be able to prepare and practice these attributes in marriage. This was the case with my husband. He was okay with the hardships, with no desire to bring thrill and excitement to the relation. We did not communicate about the discrepancies our relationship was witnessing.

We can't change people, and we have to accept them the way they are. We are not the ones to mould them in a shape that we like, instead, we have control over ourselves, and we can adjust the frames accordingly. We have to dissect our happiness from the provided circumstances. We should not focus on what people think about us. Why waste so much energy for such aimless thought?

Do you think people get separated and break up any relationship because there is no love? No, this is not the only reason. The relation's roots are never strong since the beginning, and we start building a framework on such weak grounds. How do you expect it to result in a firm model? The relationship in a marriage is strong and fragile at the same time. If there is mutual understanding where both participants love, respect and care for each other, it will grow stronger with time. Trust is the main ingredient. On the contrary, if there are differences and no acceptance, it will never add any value to the relation. I have experienced the same in my marriage.

You should accept the fact that love and respect can't be forced and imposed on anyone. These are naturally developed in our hearts. I suggest you see in the surroundings, and you will observe many weak marriages, where the couple lives in a forceful relation and spend the precious years of their life in frustration and unnatural happiness. The world considers them 'ideal', seeing the number of years of their togetherness. What it seems may not be the truth. You do not know their side of the story. An abusive relationship can never guarantee a happy life, and it is not wise to live in a toxic relationship for the sake of culture or community.

Naturally, we idealise a lot about our life partners by expecting them to be '*perfect*' – an illusion that makes us happy. We expect they would have an ocean of love and respect for us. When we fail to find these qualities in them, we start hating our personality as we think we don't deserve it. We fight with our choices.

Do you know what is worse? It's when our relationships are failing, and we never dig into the root cause of it. We blame our traits for that and prefer to go for therapy, go away from our partners, or go to couple counselling. We find ways for bringing back peace in our lives, even if it requires us to travel out of the place we live in. At that time only, we focus on what makes us happy. The decisions might help us in these times, but they fail our relationships in the long run.

We don't sit with each other to find out the toxicities that are ruining our intimacy, and this is the actual solution.

"Finding happiness is like finding yourself. You don't find happiness, you make happiness. You choose happiness. Self-actualisation is a process of discovering who you are, who you want to be and paving the way to happiness by doing what brings you the most meaning and contentment to your life over the long run."

-David Leonhardt

The time when I got lost wondering with all my memories and let my thoughts flow from my fingertip is the time when I chose to write this book. My life experiences compelled me to write this and let people know, life is hard, but it will never remain the same. The mistakes I made by devaluing myself because people had always let me down, I don't want anyone to consider their valuable self as meaningless. I was let down by the people I devoted my time to, but they never appreciated me. I was weak to retaliate and started feeling comfortable with everything thrown at me. I considered it was my duty to live a life full of obligations, unrealistic demands that demeaned me and always thought this is it!

I never took out time to look in the mirror for how I was treating my life. Until my well-wishers told me that this

64

wasn't healthy, I never understood it, and I never realised that it was my job to take care of myself. I was not created to go with the flow, where there was no love, happiness, and respect served to me even after giving it all to my family and my husband, mainly.

I learned a lesson with the experience when you need to fly again, strengthen your broken trust and get emotional support. Empty words and thoughts mean nothing. Actions show the actual results, and if you want to bring a change in something, you have to take 'control' of it. Be brave to take responsibility to make yourself happy by putting yourself above all, and move forward. Don't seize your speed. Keep walking until you are near to the destination, that is, *'self-actualisation'*.

"The purpose of life is to know yourself, create yourself, and experience yourself as 'Who You Really Are'. There is no other reason to do anything."

-Neale Donald Walsch

You will always find people criticising you, pushing you back and bringing hurdles in your way. It's all in your hands what you focus on – the limitations which others create, or to keep walking on the road you chose for your success. Take out some time from your schedule and understand what fears and anxieties you have in your life. Work on them to bring the best person in you. Prioritise working out on them, keeping in view the importance and urgency, one by one.

When you control your emotions and get a hold of the root cause of your problems, you only become wise. Every moment you spend worrying about the past, or keep a grudge for a person, or fear the incontrollable, you lose the precious time you could have invested in creating happiness. I urge you. There's no reason for not being happy. All you have to do is to let go of the past, cherish the memories it gave and take lessons from the experience it gave.

"Don't waste your time in anger, regrets, worries, and grudges. Life is too short to be unhappy."

-Roy T. Bennett

When I was spending my days in the struggle to find a shelter and earn a living, there were several times when I lost my calm, and I broke down, but I had those beautiful people around me who only brought the positive in me. I know it would be a little difficult for you initially to have self-control, but once you have a command of it, you will help others as well. Never lose hope in the dark times. They will not last forever.

There will be sunrise which will bring hope, love and new chances. You will get surprises each day about the potential you have in yourself if you start loving yourself and happy in the present moment. Do not waste your time giving ear to people who only show you the weaknesses you have. Focus and surround yourself with positive people, but never depend on them for your happiness.

Conclusion

The lesson of this chapter is that we should never expect others to make us happy. In any relationship, it should be a two-way understanding to spread love and respect, else the weak relationship will not live longer. By pushing behind all fears and insecurities, we should focus on the positive sides that naturally makes us happy inside out. If we trust others with a key to our happiness treasure, we will always get disappointment in return. It's our life, and we should have control over it.

No one else should be given the chance and permission to devalue our self-esteem and make us insecure. In relationships, too, happiness is never a one-sided process. It's an effort that both partners should put in. However, we should not depend on others to make us happy. Love and respect can't be forced and materialised. Spread love more often to the world. It needs it!

"You will never be happy if you continue to search for what happiness consists of. You will never live if you are looking for the meaning of life."

- Albert Camus

Chapter 6: Discover All There Is to Life

"I believe that each of us is born with a life purpose."

-Jack Canfield

'Life begins at the end of your comfort zone'. We hear this saying whenever we experience an unpromising situation in our lives where our expectations are hurt – from people, from our own goals, and the circumstances around us. Most of the time, we don't know about our life purpose and trust me, there is no age limit to find the goal.

There are people, who are sure what they want to do in life just in their 20s, and there are people, too, who go with the flow without any purpose, and after years of dealing with life, they find one purpose. Don't worry. There are also the types who spend the life and don't really live it. It's okay not to have any purpose, but it's not okay to waste a precious life on useless chores.

Life is an unpredictable playground where we step in with our preparations and think we are all set to go. We have made our strategies before the game and a clear mindset of 'winning' only.

"If life were predictable it would cease to be life, and be without flavor."

-Eleanor Roosevelt

Do you worry about the 'purpose' of your life? Let's do an exercise. Take some time out from your day, every day, and think about the world. How does it look like to you? What are the areas which need improvements, and what could possibly be the role that you can play to bring a change? You will get an answer by having a clue of something your interest. You will discover an inspiration to contribute to making the world better along with having the best version of your life. This should be your *'purpose'*.

I have been emphasising the importance of positivity and interacting with positive people. Life is nothing but a test, and it is very important to be prepared for the result. We can only try our best and attempt to score the highest, but we never know what life holds for us despite our hard work and efforts. We can't be winners all the time.

We plan, and we prepare according to our plans so that we achieve our desired goals. We make ourselves focused on the positive side, which we assume, is success only. Let me tell you, the definition of success varies from person to person, but in a general sense, I call it 'not failing even after falling'.

"If you set your goals ridiculously high and it's a failure, you will fail above everyone else's success."

-James Cameron

We know life is uncertain, and there are times when our patience is tested hard, we fail to understand the meaning of life because we lose our direction and forget the purpose. As we grow older, we should become wiser, but everyone's life is different for every adult. The way we see it, life would be different from someone who has never seen success, or from someone who has no one in his life as emotional support, or who has it all will have a different mindset.

I told you earlier. People should never be considered as a 'commodity'. They breathe, they have emotions, and they have feelings. No person has a right to use someone for their benefit and then discard them.

People associated with us have their own rights and values. We can't control them. Often, the relations associated with us think they have the authority to control us, while this is inhumane. Human beings are born free. They have their identities and their choices. No one has the right to direct them for anything.

We don't have control over our own plans either. There is a Jewish saying: "*When humans plan things, God is laughing.*" This refers to the power of humans in comparison with the power of God, who's the supreme authority! We plan, but unless there is no will of God, we can never succeed, no matter how fool-proof plans are on our plates.

"Life is what happens when you're busy making other plans."

-John Lennon

We are living in a very fragile world, a chaotic life, but one thing is for sure, it is very exciting. There are surprises each day, which makes life an interesting journey. We experience happiness, sorrows, hardships and opportunities, yet we never stop moving on. We must not stop chasing our purpose, even if the situations are not favourable for us. We should be thankful for the present we have.

Imagine your future life, how it looks like to be perfect? A well-maintained house, a settled job and a happy family. What are you doing with having all the perfections? Are you settled there, or you are still worrying about the future because you have made new goals and set new standards (say purpose)? This is a self-therapy to continuously improvise yourself, align your habits to achieve your goals and never stop you grow higher.

There's a drawback to this, too. Do you know what's that? You will never be satisfied with what you have. You will only become a machine that keeps producing more and more without taking a rest. This is a form of thanklessness. You will never have enough if you keep setting your standards higher every single time. Be thankful for what you have NOW, the future is not promised to anyone,

"If you look at what you have in life, you'll always have more. If you look at what you don't have in life, you'll never have enough."

-Oprah Winfrey

There is so much life brings in for us, and we only focus on what suits us, while the other flavours have their unique tastes. We sometimes neglect them as they do not suit our taste buds, but that's what life is all about. We have to make compromises and, sometimes, sacrifices. There's a cost of everything, and that depends on our level of tolerance.

I have done this. I have accepted every lemon which life has thrown at me. I never gave up, and trust me, If I could do it, we all can do it. We all can take risks, change paths, but the target should be not to lose the direction and purpose. There are people who are always clear on their purpose from day one. They plan accordingly and make their moves according to situations. On the contrary, there are people who persistently develop their interests after observing what life offers them. I think I am the latter one. My life was never perfect, you know, the childhood I spent and the struggles I went through in my life, hence, I had to tune myself according to the given situations. I 'made' my life. It wasn't an easy journey of self-exploration, though.

Do you notice if people are associated with you to achieve their benefits? It's simple to explore. If someone is with you when you are prospering and leaves you when you have nothing, it simply means there's some benefit associated with which you can't entertain when you have nothing. I often felt that people in my life, such as my friends and acquaintances, loved me for what I had *to offer*. They purposely loved me for their own benefit.

Everyone has a different benefit. Some might love you for the beauty they see in me, others would like you for the honest nature, whereas there would be many people who would like you for materialistic reasons, such as your settled job, growing wealth, fame among the fellows, or a lavish lifestyle. Besides these people, you will find a person who genuinely admires you for just the person you are.

I always thought I should trust people for how they treat me, and the intentions they show are genuinely from their hearts. I always needed their affirmation for my actions, to know if I am going steadily, but I knew at some point I would have to draw a line. I realised it after getting betrayals from those who showed their sincerity and after experiencing a failed marriage. At some point, I was so burnout that I felt the life ended there. I didn't see any positivity, I didn't have many friends, and I was only seeing the darkness in front of me. It took me some time to realise there's always a dawn after a dark night. I learned eventually that life is more than what it seems to be.

There are endless possibilities. When everything falls apart, it's more likely falling into places, but we never wait for the opportunities ahead of us. We are always in a hurry to make things happen and then realise nothing is in our control. There are battles inside our heads for what it is and how it should be, and there are obstacles in front of us too.

In all the chaos, we are left with our thoughts and options. I have gone through this, and at that time, I only did what I thought was the best. I fought with reality checks that no one in the world is truly there for you, no one can promise to stay forever and take you out from your miseries, but you and the Almighty! I always trusted that God is there, even if I am left alone in the world, I have God with me. I always believed that God was watching over me.

Life is cruel, and if we do not make the right decisions about the people to keep them or away from our life, the people can be a 'test' too. There are times when we are left alone by the most trusted ones, we are betrayed by those we love the most, and when we have to make some harsh decisions of staying alone than in a bad company. I have been lonely many times, and then I realised I have no one except God. It was my faith that He would never leave me alone.

"All I have seen teaches me to trust the Creator for all I have not seen."

-Ralph Waldo Emerson

I knew, if God was there to give me strength and hope, nothing could let me down. I could fight the loneliness and overcome the anxiety and fears, especially the fear of not having my loved ones, my family and friends around me. This thought itself is very killing if you ever give it a moment to ponder. When you need someone to be your emotional support or a shoulder to lean on, and then you find there is not a single person available to comfort you.

I felt this pain, but deep down, I had the faith that God is always there to love me, comfort me and reward me for all the hardships. I knew my life would become harder with each passing day, but I had this contentment of faith in my heart. I trusted God with my destiny, that is why I handed over my worries in His hands and felt a lot less burdened.

When was the last time you felt scared to take a step because you had the gut feeling to be failed? I felt scared many times in life, and this is absolutely normal. Bringing change in life is not that simple. It is a whole new renovation. The first step towards anything is always the hardest. There are insecurities, doubts, shattering confidence and a high level of demotivation, but hold on to it because you will succeed. Once you achieve something in life against all odds, the view from the top is beautiful.

I have made some mistakes by not taking the right step at the right time. I don't want you to make such a mistake. Learn to take a stand for yourself when you know you are right. There will be suppressive behaviours and oppressive people who would overwhelm you every single time. Always have a strong voice to speak for what's true and for yourself. It will save you from the regret of not raising the voice for the right when you had all the capacity and power.

Family is gifted by nature, but you are independent to choose your friends. Always try to make such friends who sync with your mindset and life's vision, who brighten your dark days through their words and presence, who motivate and encourage you, and most importantly, the people who make you believe that you MATTER. Keep including more positive people. I keep on saying this because the company you keep shapes you for your future. The kindness people bring to our lives go a long way.

I firmly believe that whenever we experience the feeling of 'guilt' about something, it is only because we limit the powers we have in ourselves – the power to overhaul the situation, to create happiness, and to accept life as it is. Don't allow any guilt to reside in your heart.

Conclusion

In this chapter, we learned that life is never ideal for everyone. It becomes challenging at times, but the aim should be to keep going. We have the power to take out the positive from life's hurdles, and we have the capacity to create a purpose at any point. Positivity, kind people and their motivation always lift us up, therefore, we should make this a 'goal' too to surround ourselves with good people, a positive environment and a clear goal. There's always something that life holds for us. We only have to discover the goal persistently until we have a good and healthy lifestyle. It is never too late to start working on yourself. Bring in the energy, which requires replacing the weaknesses with strengths. Start from somewhere. Start right now.

"You have the power to achieve greatness and create anything you want in life, but you must take action."

-Jack Canfield

Chapter 7: Always Know That Life Has No Simple Answers

But at the end of the day, there are some questions that have no answers, and then one answer that has no question: love rules the game. Every time. All the time. That's what counts.

-James McBride

I have been talking about life and how we should deal with every situation we experience. I advised you to adjust in life in a way that does not harm your inner peace. When you can't change the environment, you have to mould yourself flexibly to fit in the requirements of the surroundings. You should be careful with your actions with people, but also, first, you should love and take care of yourself. Only then you will be able to spread happiness to your surroundings.

We have discussed that no one can take responsibility for the happiness of others. In life, we have to make several harsh decisions so that we can grow and move forward. Change comes from taking risks, and it can only occur if we dare to take realistic decisions. There should be no place for guilt or regret in hearts. Remember, you should never justify anything you did to secure your present or future.

"We can believe what we choose. We are answerable for what we choose to believe."

-John Henry Newman

It is not right to justify your actions constantly because you have an equal right to exist and to love yourself without doing anything for others. You were born free, and self-care is your basic right. You can do anything that makes you happy. No one should question this.

As I said earlier, life always throws lemon on us, and it is up to us what we make out of it. Life can never be simple. It will never give us multiple chances to make the most of any opportunity. In my opinion, this is what makes life beautiful and thrilling when we receive surprises from it and redirect our paths.

We come across difficult questions when we *self-reflect*. The questions that may arise in our mind and confuse us could be:

- *Am I doing my best?*
- *Am I grateful for this life?*
- *Should I really care about society?*
- *What if I don't have any goals?*
- *Will I still achieve anything in life?*
- *Why so many hardships when I trust God?*
- *Does He not love me?*
- *Do moral values really exist?*
- *What does my future hold for me? etc... etc...*

There are times when we are not able to make any decision because we don't realise how it will result. We make plans in our lives and assume it will result as we expect because we work on it the way we want. However, it happens that we do not get the desired results, and here, we lose focus on our purpose.

Distraction kills the motive to do something meaningful in life, but we never know what life has for us ahead even if we lose our direction.

"Sometimes it takes a wrong turn to get you to the right place."

-Mandy Hale

There are times when we do not have any particular direction in mind because we do not know what we want to achieve. We just go with the flow. We realise the necessity to bring change only when we go through and make decisions. It's risky, but it is exciting too. The unknown destinations have more surprises than a planned trip.

In life, you can't always go with the flow only. Otherwise, there would be no charm in leading a boring life. Life is all about thrilling and unexpected turns, which challenge us in every possible manner. We know our worth only in uncontrollable situations with lesser choices. This is when you know what you want and what you have to do for it.

When the results are in our favour, it will boost our morale, but we can only fulfil our expectations when we take responsibility for our actions and the outcomes. I will urge again. Our prime responsibility must be to love ourselves before anyone.

Our strong faith helps us to pass through any situation. I told you earlier, I had a hard life, but what kept me moving was my faith in God. I knew He was taking care of me. I could not see Him, but I could see the transformations in my life from rags to a rich, independent woman.

God is the purest example of love. He blesses us immensely, no matter how good or bad we are. He knows what's in our hearts for each other.

"God is God. He knows what he is doing. When you can't trace his hand, trust his heart."

-Max Lucado

We can hide our intent from the world, but Almighty knows us the best. We should not forget that He has created us. Many of us will have good intentions for others, and some people may be hiding evil desires, but He never rewards us on the basis of our desires.

He tests us from hardships as well as ease too, and on the basis of our actions and treatment of others, He brings in the consequences. We can never judge God's will, neither can we understand His judiciousness.

The difficulties or ease that we go through are already written in our destiny by God. Human beings are the noblest of creation, which is why we are tested and rewarded the most, too. We are much stronger than we think. God has designed our journeys and destination in life, and He knows how to take us there.

In my life, I did not have a clear path. I only trusted the Almighty to *go with the flow*. God always blessed me with an inner power to deal with the unforeseen hurdles coming my way, and my unmoved faith in God always helped me to get through all obstacles victoriously.

How I Dealt With the Hard Times

You know that I went through a lot of hardships throughout my life. There were days, which I call the most terrifying, depressing and darkest. Those were the days when my emotions were numbed. I had no money in hand to bear my daily expenses. I did not have any proper shelter or even a room. In the chilling winters, I had no support to keep myself warm.

All I was provided with was a basement of my work. I had no other choice. It was an inexplicably toughest time. I discussed this with my boss that I had never seen such an all-time lowest phase in my life before. At that time, I had many questions which did not have any answers, or at least, I was not able to figure out if ever I would be able to get out of this life.

My hardships were not only limited to 'no shelter', but I was also going through emotional turmoil. My marriage was breaking up, and I was heading towards separation. There was no chance for me to stop and cry over all this. No, I had to go through this without giving up. At that point, God did His miracle and sent some precious people into my life who made it worth struggling. They were my guiding angels, who made a hard time a little easier to survive.

"We see God's miracles in His wondrous work and in our own personal lives."

-Neil L. Andersen

The kindness and love they showed had brightened up my life and helped me a lot to fight with the circumstances, which, at that time, seemed impossible, but I chose to keep going. My life started to change eventually. I shifted from the basement to a proper hostel, where I had a designated place to sleep fearlessly in any kind of season. I kept hustling for temporary accommodations because I was striving to improve my lifestyle and never wanted to fail myself.

Hard times test your patience, but also, they bring the most patient person in you, which you only realised when you are left with a situation with no solution. It becomes a *'do or die'* condition, and tell me, who would choose to die then? We don't fight the hard times. We fight for life.

Hard Decisions Are Important!

There are times in life when we make decisions of disinterest because we have to use the provided resources when dealing with a situation. We use our intellect to make a move that is reasonable according to the situation. We know this is not what we want, but our determination is to liberate ourselves and make peace with our present. For this, we have to make hard decisions by following our intuition, even if they are at the cost of our relations, or a job, or anything close to our hearts. If peace lies in going away from them, we should move forward and create an ideal environment for us.

"You've got to make tough decisions, sometimes unpopular decisions... Whatever it is, if it's the right move at the right time, you've got to be also willing to make mistakes."

-Sean McDermott

It is okay to doubt yourself for a mistake after making the right decision, but it is not okay to make a wrong decision and stay with it. Temporary suffering is better than enduring agony. To err is human, and it's okay to make mistakes. They only polish us for bigger battles, and there is always something to learn from the mistakes if we observe.

People Are Selfish!

People are not what they appear to us. The way people treat us speaks volumes about them. I told you, people should not be considered commodities to be used and then thrown afterwards. They should be handled with love, care and kindness. What I have dealt with in life is the opposite. People use each other for their own benefit. They lie and manipulate us so that their needs are satisfied through us.

Remember, people do not lie because of you or for you. The lies are for their own interests. It could be a glittery truth for the world, but what they speak is merely their *'self-deception'*. They want to believe something, which isn't true. They find pleasure in making others guilty for something impractical. That simply means they are lying to themselves for their own benefit.

Don't Get Manipulated!

The world is a cruel place. While we are searching for answers to our own questions, and as we are busy making difficult decisions out of our comfort zone, there are people who want to control others according to their choices. They manipulate others and create such scenarios, which are a betrayal in disguise.

I object to such a mindset, and I oppose anyone oppressing others by any means. I have witnessed people doing manipulative acts to someone who's progressing in life. There can be multiple reasons:

They want a reaction from you:

People want to learn, what our weaknesses are so that they can use them against us, whenever required. They observe how we react if they do or say something offensive. Through this, they would get to know how to create hurdles for us in moving forward. Don't let their reactions affect you. It's as simple as that!

They think you are owned by them:

One of the most significant reasons for manipulation is the idealism of controlling someone. This gives a superiority complex to some people, I am sure. People feel above everyone else when they know they have control over someone's decisions, actions and overall life. Never forget, you are your own master, don't allow anyone to control you.

If you don't react to it, they let you know with shame and fear:

The great art is to ignore what people try to do to let you down. I have learned that a NO reply is a powerful reply for any lies that people say, their manipulations, and controlling behaviours.

It gave me inner peace, and I want to pass this advice on to you. If you don't react, it becomes a shame for people because they never expected that. This will weaken their false powers and save you from being manipulated.

They try to make you fearful and guilty:

People impose their manipulative behaviours on you so that you feel the obligation that you HAVE to be the way they expect. You HAVE to help them at the cost of your own peace. Let me tell you, such obligations make you weak. You will fear that if you fail to meet people's expectations, they will be hurt.

This makes you feel guilty, and hence, the purpose of people's manipulation succeeds by diverting you from your path. It's in your hands NOT to allow anyone to make you feel any guilt for something unreal.

You choose to use truth and logic whereas they don't:

I believe in the power of truth. No matter how many lies have been spoken, how bad the situation has been made for us, or how manipulative the world becomes towards us, it's the *'truth'* that wins in the end.

If you tackle any manipulation with facts and logic, no one can overpower you. Trust me on this. All you need to do is stay steadfast on your path and not allow anyone to disturb the peace of your mind. Your truth is your power against every lie. You are much stronger than you think, and this is your biggest success, that is, a confident mindset.

Conclusion

In this chapter, we learned that life never comes easy to us, and it is not always necessary that we get all the answers to the questions we encounter in our journey. There are times when we have to make hard decisions for our progression. Here again, the people we are surrounded with play an important role in going through rough patches of life. Also, there are people who manipulate us for their own benefit. We should not trust anyone easily just for the words they say. Be observant!

Chapter 8: Shed People Off and Keep Going

"If you're going to try, go all the way. Otherwise, don't even start. This could mean losing girlfriends, wives, relatives and maybe even your mind. It could mean not eating for three or four days. It could mean mockery-- isolation. Isolation is the gift... If you're going to try, go all the way. There is no other feeling like that. You will be alone with the gods, and the nights will flame with fire. You will ride life straight to perfect laughter. It's the only good fight there is."

-Charles Bukowski

The funny thing about life is that it is a seesaw ride, which ideally expects us to ride through the highs and lows both with courage and a smile on our faces. And you know what? That is indeed the best way to both the highs and the lows. Let's say you got a promotion. It is naturally easy to be happy and believe in the bounty of life, and look ahead to the good times. But what about when a loved one walks out of your life? The pain can be like your own limb has been cut off. How do you move on from a loss such as this?

The Most Painful Kind of Loss

I call the pain of losing people the most painful kind of loss because it's not just a person walking out of your life. It's a collection of memories walking out, taking away a part of your essence and soul. The curious thing about this kind of loss is that it is universal, found everywhere, in everyone.

I can bet that nobody reading this chapter can say that I have not lost anyone in life. Go ahead, reflect deeply into your life if you think so. You will remember times, yes, multiple instances, where people that you hoped and believed would stay with you throughout your life left you. Either they left wilfully or got lost at the hands of circumstances. Out of these two scenarios, let us consider the former.

What is the most immediate reaction you feel when a loved one moves out of your life? It strikes the heart as excruciatingly as a slap of rejection. The worst of the worst is when people leave you when you need them the most. In that circumstance, the emotion streaming through you is that of disappointment too. You will wallow in despair, will be found at the bottom of a bottle, will cry tears and may isolate yourself from the world... and you know what, for a while, that is fine.

Deep losses do deserve their deserving periods of mourning. Grief, when done right, can be healthy for us emotionally and psychologically. It also tells you something about the beauty of your heart that you loved someone fully.

But there eventually comes a time when you have to accept that the person is gone and will not return. That is where you have to gradually escape that shell and look behind your back to find wings. You will have to accept that life has not ended and that much more remains, in terms of experiences, in terms of goal fulfilment, and meeting new people yet. I always live by this quote by Anne Lamott:

"You will lose someone you can't live without, and your heart will be badly broken, and the bad news is that you never completely get over the loss of your beloved. But this is also the good news. They live forever in your broken heart that doesn't seal back up. And you come through. It's like having a broken leg that never heals perfectly—that still hurts when the weather gets cold, but you learn to dance with the limp."

-Anne Lamott

Moving On

I asked you to reflect on your life and think about the people you lost. Now I want you to think back to those losses and reflect on the moving on process. In particular, I want you to think about the new people you found after having lost the old ones.

To tell you the truth, this is indeed the way of the world. You lose one person, the universe compensates by granting you another. It's a strange kind of cosmic balance that will at all costs maintain its equilibrium. It's the nature of this world that we learn when we grow older and gather more experience. By this accord, the experience of loss then becomes a blessing in the long run, no?

About this cosmic balance, one of the most influential poets wrote the following:

"Don't grieve. Anything you lose comes round in another form."

-Rumi

And this is truer than true!

After you lose loved ones, you will be compensated by those who may actually be there for you without expecting you to pay back anything at all. In other words, you will find better connections. All you would require when going through the abyss of loss will be patience. They call it a 'virtue' for good reasons.

Through Faith

We cannot erase the possibility that, for some people, losses can be too heavy. Some people may lose a number of people in quick succession or all at once, for whatever reasons. Some people may not even have that many people in life. These people keep a small company of as many as one, two or three really close people.

To people such as these, loss and grief hits harder, hits differently. Especially if you are someone who spent a great many years building and nurturing these few people close to you. In such a case, the shock and despair of losing the loved one can hit you like an axe.

I will, in all honesty, assure you that I have been one of those who did not have anybody at one point in time. I lost everyone I once had faith and belief in and ended up lonely. Only one strategy helped me in such a place, and that will be the strategy I shall recommend to you: faith in God or any higher power.

"Faith is not the belief that God will do what you want. It is the belief that God will do what is right."

-Max Lucado,

See, at one point in time, so many catastrophes took place in my life that, one by one, I lost everyone. You would naturally think that I was smothered by grief to the point that I could not function. Believe it or not, but that is not true. Why? Because God never left my hand. He was always there for me, within me, around me, above me. His presence was all that I needed, and so in praying to Him and supplicating from Him, I got all the consolation and courage I needed.

I always felt there is and will always be so much for me to face in life. I knew that the circumstances could get worse than they were, but I knew I would win at some point because I had the Almighty watching over me. My faith was strong. I also found the consolation that God had something special planned for me in the losses that I experienced. That indeed turned out to be the truth.

So, no matter what religion, faith or belief you associate with, whether you believe in God or some vague kind of higher power, know that something out there is looking out for you. Reach out to it. Perhaps nothing but intuition will help you grasp that entity, but you know that something is there. Do not be crippled with fear and sorrow. Trust in the plans that the God, universe, nature, and cosmic force have laid out for you. As someone beautifully said:

"Never be afraid to trust an unknown future to a known God."

-Corrie ten Boom

Once you do that, you will transcend all the obstacles placed in your life. You will be out of pain like a strand of hair out of butter. You have the helping hand of God, the truest and the most concerned friend in your life.

The Conquerable Nature of Negative Emotions

"Depression, anger, and sadness are states of mind, and so are happiness, peace, and contentment. You can choose to be in any of these states because it's your mind."

-Maddy Malhotra

Many people I have seen and talked to consider their emotions as absolute. It is as if there is something final within what they feel that they allow it to take over.

Guilt, anxiety, hatred, shame, grief. As we discussed, to some extent, allowing one to feel these emotions and come clear through them is something that is very normal. If you have been someone who has been investing too much of themselves in other people – for example, sacrificed your happiness for their sake – the depth and dimensions of these emotions will attack deeper.

I want to assure you, though, that sometimes things in our life that do not work out for you have absolutely nothing to do with you. If you are honest with yourself in your self-reflection, you will agree with me here. Relationships such as marriage require two people to make it work. But sometimes, despite both people being good human beings individually, they just can't make it work when they come together. We may have no control over such matters. All our life, we have heard that things in life just go bad, and more importantly, bad things happen to good people.

Have you ever wondered what should you do after having acknowledged such a truth? Do you know what the way out of these 'divine injustices' done to you is? Taking control of your emotions. As Maddy Malhotra has written above, these emotions are but states of mind. Like a switch, you can choose which state you want to be in.

You see, God is not exactly a cruel God. Yes, he does test His people, but he tests them according to their capacity. Therefore, if you are going through some kind of loss or major grief, know that God wants you to work on something. It could be that God realises that your grief-coping mechanism needs fine-tuning, so He may make someone you love dearly walk out of your life. It could be anything since God truly works in mysterious ways. Your goal is to have faith in the process and making sure that you are in control of your mind.

I cannot emphasise how vital it is for us to not allow ourselves to come under the influence of our mind, and especially the negative emotions it throws at us. Rather, our mind should serve as our servant. We should be in the driving seat, otherwise, we will keep crashing into this building or that signage.

At every step and stage of your life, you have to be self-aware of your emotions and take control of them. We have talked so much about putting yourself first and loving yourself. Taking control of your emotions and mind is indeed an act of loving yourself and doing what's best for you.

Conclusion

In this chapter, we talked about the most painful kind of loss there is – of losing people. As we saw, it is okay to feel sad, guilty, scared, but for the time being only. It is not okay to carry the grudge in you for your entire life, and it is best for you to accept the reality of the situation. Any other way of living is a toxic lifestyle, at least in my opinion.

For each person, grief takes a toll accordingly. Some people invest more in people. Some have a very limited number of close ones in their life. At the end of the day, when nothing else works, we must hold on to faith. What's necessary for life is to look at the thorn and trust that the rose will appear. That is faith, and faith requires patience to manifest.

Many times, you will have to take control of your mind and emotions. Emotions are nothing but states of mind. They are not absolute. Therefore, ensure that you are in control of them and not the other way around. In the end, your goal in life is to move on and learn from whatever kind of experience there is that greets you along the way.

Chapter 9: Moving On and Celebrating Yourself

"You can spend minutes, hours, days, weeks, or even months over-analysing a situation; trying to put the pieces together, justifying what could've, would've happened... or you can just leave the pieces on the floor and move the fuck on."

-Tupac Shakur

In the grand scheme of things, when the dust of the present calamities have settled, and you move above and beyond the inhibitions and horridness of the present situation, the only thing that will have served you well when you look back is having moved forward.

The Bliss of Moving Forward and Starting Anew

See, good and bad situations are part of every being's life. Everyone experiences it. Every. Single. Person. If it bursts your bubble, so be it, but the truth is that your hardships are not so unique. No, the universe is not set out to hunt you. No, you are not the special godforsaken one. No, pessimism is not supposed to be your revenge against people and life.

What then are you supposed to do about your not-so-unique, not-so-horrible hardships? (By no means do I mean to invalidate your experiences, I just am giving a ray of hope). The same thing that the most driven and aspiring beings on earth do... Move on. Look forward. Look ahead.

If one thing is common in all of our lives, it's a hardship. We get that. But there are moments of joy and wonder and beauty too. Hardships will come and go, like every other sentiment in life. Then why give it as much weight? Why let it hold you back and weigh you down? It's part of living, and I know how hard it gets, believe me. You feel paralysed, rather like you're in a quagmire, and the only way feels to be down. But the truth is, things sure get better when you look forward to letting go and moving on.

This means creating life with a new free faith and hope, strength and dignity. For moving on, starting over is the most crucial thing. As the saying goes:

"Sometimes the hardest part isn't letting go but rather learning to start over."

-Nicole Sobon

By starting anew, I do not mean that you live your life from scratch. Simply that you pick up the responsibilities, obligations, desires where you left them off and re-evaluate what each of these means to you. Once you do that, your vigour will return, and you will feel the joy of living again.

Look Within and Choose Yourself

So, you can start with what importance does work hold in your life? (Answers could be: it earns me money, brings food to the table, I support my family through it, it makes me and my abilities feel useful and lucrative). Ask yourself about your education; why am I studying what I am studying? (It's something that I am interested in, it will help me secure a career in the future, I feel happy learning about my particular discipline. Ask yourself about freedom, about your family, about your passions, and find the courage and drive to work hard towards them again.

We human beings are strange creatures. We can *choose* to love each other intensely, love our spouse and our children faithfully and unconditionally, but seldom do we extend that privilege towards ourselves. We never strive to become our own best friend, our own lover, our own mother and child.

Can you imagine how many negativities and toxic traits we would let go of if we just choose to love ourselves and talk to us and advise us like we would our loved one? Can you imagine how much control will that bring to your life, how much maturity, and by being well-aware of yourself, you will be knowledgeable about others too. You will be able to deal with their emotions, moods, dialogues, etc.

All of this comes from the desire to move on from the harsher experiences in life. Don't let them define you, rather define yourself on your own terms. Based on your love and trust towards yourself. Once you start to do that, you will learn and remember to always trust your feelings. You will develop a connection with your intuition and will know that your hunches are always right. Always.

Don't Fear the Fall – Fear Not Trying.

While I am hyping it up, I know it is really difficult to let go, move on and start anew. It will worry us. We will set out to do good for ourselves and others, but we will stumble and fall. Sometimes we will make months of progress to only have it ultimately crumble one day, God forbid. But will you begrudge yourself? Will you insist on feeling terrible about yourself, gloat and turn sour? Or will you do the right thing:

"Grudges are for those who insist that they are owed something; forgiveness, however, is for those who are substantial enough to move on."

-Criss Jami

Vow to yourself to forgive yourself for your future transgressions and stumbles.

See, we have all the possibilities. We may fall, but we may fly as well! If we fall, the only thing to do is to forgive

102

ourselves and… surprise surprise, move on again! And if we fly? Well, then we only have to reach and ascend higher and higher. Such is the beauty of life.

Drift With Your Dreams

I have seen a banana vendor selling his bananas, trying to send his children to school. I have seen the people working as garbage carriers in Africa with hopes and aspirations. People like us don't have that life, at least I don't. Yet, I have known myself to bemoan my circumstances and cry over spilt milk.

You and I have so many more possibilities given our education and experiences. We have reaped the rewards for choosing to be a little patient and determined, have we not? Being ambitious in life, becoming an independent person does nothing but serve us for the future. Hope is our personal miracle, our messiah, our holy grail. We are wonderful creatures who can weave our destiny by just setting our minds on something and choosing to stay in the direction of that fearlessly and adamantly until we succeed.

You must have many goals in life too, don't you? You may now be wallowing, but look within the library of yourself and bring out those favourite books that have gathered dust due to neglect. What are you doing about those goals and dreams? Do you not believe in them, or do you not think that you can achieve those things?

I guarantee you. You would go very far by focusing on your goals. Be led by them rather than by people and what they say. Be led by your ambitions rather than wallowing in self-pity. Be led by action rather than inaction. Be led by dreaming than simply sleeping. You have tried all latter things, have they served you? Why not try the right way, then? What have you got to lose?

I want you to choose your happiness over everything else. There is a difference between a smart job and a happy job. I chose to go with what makes me happy, and that has worked wonders for me. Whatever hindrance lies in your way to be happy or content, get it out. Sometimes it may be very small, like in the story The Princess and the Pea. A little pea could be causing you deep, sleepless troubles. I want you to release it all!

"Even though you may want to move forward in your life, you may have one foot on the brakes. In order to be free, we must learn how to let go. Release the hurt. Release the fear. Refuse to entertain your old pain. The energy it takes to hang onto the past is holding you back from a new life. What is it you would let go of today?"

-Mary Manin Morrissey

Anxiety as a Hindrance

On the path of letting go and starting new, you will encounter many anxious individuals looking to change their lives. They are riddled with the what-if questions and fears.

When you meet someone suffering from anxiety, our instinct is to give advice to that person. They don't need advice at that point. When we give them that, it's like we're bringing water for someone who isn't thirsty, who didn't even ask for water.

What an anxious person needs is someone to just listen. Anxious people want to be heard. They are holding things within that need release. Let them speak of how they feel.

When you talk about a solution with them, you make it about yourself. Strange as it may sound, advising in that situation maybe stemming from a place of a saviour complex. Or you are just desperate to help the person. The medicine you are using is wrong, though. As Anais Nin said:

"Anxiety is love's greatest killer. It makes others feel as you might when a drowning man holds on to you. You want to save him, but you know he will strangle you with his panic."

-Anais Nin

You will feel strangled if you try to give advice to someone suffering from anxiety. This is why I say, just hear the person out.

Anxiety is a strong part of encountering change. And changing your circumstances to evolve from then, move on and starting anew is bound to bring in anxiety. It is, therefore, best to just find a listening ear and let it all out.

Celebrate Yourself

You are an awesome individual. It'll just be a shame if you don't celebrate yourself.

Last year in 2020, for a couple of months straight, I faced plenty of fear and ample job rejections. Had I worried and wallowed, I would have gotten stuck. But I did nothing of that sort.

I eventually got myself a job in one of the most amazing companies, nCino Global Ltd. From the moment I came across my recruiter and the rest of the process, I felt passionate about the work. Optimism paid off. I got over the grief of the failed marriage when I started focusing on my happiness and living on my own terms. That was a fresh start for me.

The Phases of Life

Life is all about securing happiness and surrounding yourself with people who love you and appreciate you. The life I have lived has taught me the following (the same may or may not apply to you):

- The 20s are the years when you usually break away from your basic education, living with your parents and seek independence.

- The 30s are the years you try to make a serious career and discover that family ghosts are living in and affecting you in many ways.

- The 40s are the years you try to get acquainted with the fact that you're getting old and may feel a crisis coming. You may start doing a lot of sports and look after your well-being.

No matter what phase of life you are in, you can move on from your past and redefine what meaning you want to give your life.

Conclusion

No matter the trials and tribulations, your attitude in life should be of seeking a new beginning. Every day is an opportunity to start fresh. Your grief of yesterdays and yesteryears don't have to carry on forever. Put a stop to it. Choose your happiness, even if it is anxiety-inducing. You will not regret it. You have dreams and goals that yearn for actualisation. Believe in yourself and make them come true. Celebrate yourself and be led by happiness.

Chapter 10: Believe In Yourself

"Believe in your infinite potential. Your only limitations are those you set upon yourself."

-Roy T. Bennett

I want to start with an example of old age to prove that you can deny the so-called facts if you change the way you look at things and believe in something better.

Getting Old vs Feeling Old

Just life hardship is inevitable in life, so is getting old. While getting old is an inevitable fact you will be facing eventually, *feeling old* is an option. The following quote rings close to this idea:

"Getting older makes you no wiser, but number of lessons you learned."

-Toba Beta

The objectivity of turning 50 or 60 or 70 should not entail that you have to feel old now too if you have reached that age. Given the lessons, you have learned and the experiences you have gathered, you have to keep the inner child alive. No matter how long your life, you still have so much left to learn. So continue to look at things in a new light. Enjoy not only Spring but also Autumn. Try to be present and live each moment to the fullest!

This is all part of believing in yourself. Since we have scarcely been trained and socialised to do that, we have to make that change ourselves.

Change Is In Our Control

We have kept talking throughout this book that change is in our control. Change is in *your* control. You saw that pain and hardships are inevitable, but if you change the way you look at them, your grief and misery will no longer be a bother. You have to change the way you look at old age in order to feel young again. This is all part of faith and belief in yourself!

It is okay to complain about circumstances and be angry, but only to get your grief out, Only for the sake of catharsis. Since things that are suppressed and left to simmer within end up revealing themselves eventually in ugly ways. So get your pain out, get your sadness out. Vent and rant as much as you like. But make it instrumental, i.e., make sure that it is a means to the end of your ultimate satisfaction. Once all the dirt is out, and catharsis is done, now is the time to change your beliefs and make the choices that will lead to greater happiness.

It takes many years and lots of love, kindness and patience to learn this. Believe me, I know. It is hard to not let your circumstances dictate where your life is going. But this is also just like thinking that the horse leads you while you have the reins to it in your hands. That perspective of a lack of control also needs to change. You need to start believing in yourself. Not many people do that, but you can since you are more aware now.

Change all your previous conditioning and live with this mentality:

"The only person who can pull me down is myself, and I'm not going to let myself pull me down anymore."

-C. Joybell C.

Don't Let People Bring You Down

It takes great courage to believe in yourself, to hold yourself as your most valuable priority and to not be swayed by others. The most harmful thing that I have seen people do is letting others' opinions torture them. It's like the quote goes:

"Your time is way too precious to be wasting on people that can't accept you for who you are."

-Turcois Ominek

Hold your head up high and be proud of yourself. People will not always like you, so what? Let them not! You love yourself, and that's enough. You respect yourself and look after your well-being. Why else does it matter then if nobody else does? Just know that you have SO much to give to yourself and then also to this world.

By no means am I saying that you should go away and live alone in solitude. I'm saying, if people don't appreciate you, let go of them. There will always be more who will appreciate you. If you don't have anyone that appreciates you, then be ALONE until you find them. The universe is not cruel. It knows what you need, and it takes its time to give you the right thing at the right time.

Like all good things, this won't be easy either, but it will make you happy. If you have yourself, you are never alone. If you believe in yourself, you will have God work miracles for you.

Seeking Self-Belief from Others

In October 2020, I made a trip to Africa and visited my family. My dad and I particularly have always shared a special bond, so I always knew that my dad was super proud of me for all my hard work, talents and my dedication towards my goals. He used to be a sailor back in the days, which influenced him to train me to become an independent person. He taught me never to give up and to just keep moving forward. Yes, a lot of lessons that I give you were passed on by my father.

He had battled for years with illness. He had fought very hard for his life, but in the October of 2020, I just knew deep down it would be my last time seeing and spending time with my dad. I had spent a memorable time with him, and it was good enough for me to know and keep my years of memories with me.

Soon after my month-long trip, I returned back. On December 6th, 2020, I got a phone call saying my dad has passed away, and that was a moment of my life where I just broke down. I had made peace within myself, or so I thought, yet I just crumbled. I was devastated. Given Christmas and New Year was ahead of us, it was the worst year of time for my dad to have passed away.

I struggled the most among my family members at his death. What kept me and keeps me going is the fact that my parents have wanted to see me happy. They have been very proud of me and believed in me. My dad was a man who worked hard, cared deeply, gave his best for people in his life. And this was a person who believed in me and would have believed in me even if nobody else had.

Therefore, I felt it incumbent upon myself to revive my self-belief thanks to the inspiration my family members provided. I let it empower me, let their belief in me add on to my own self-belief, and that has helped me soar all the more.

Conclusion

Many unpleasant things are inevitable in life: death, taxes, pain and suffering, old age. What helps us cope and still reach for success despite these hindrances is not letting these negativities bring us down. That has to do with change, and change comes from within, inspired by the belief we have cultivated in ourselves. It is for this reason that Kahlil Gibran says, "Much of our pain is self-chosen." We *choose* what we want to believe, and if that is the case, why not believe in ourselves?

People may act as a huge opposing force to your notions of self-belief. They may threaten it by bringing their opinions and judgements, but I want you to stick to the belief your loved ones have in you. Let it add with your own deposit of self-belief, and then see where that takes you.

Conclusion

"There is no real ending. It's just the place where you stop the story."

-Frank Herbert

Now that we have reached the end, I want to give a macroscopic summary of all that we talked about in this book.

We started by talking about doing what we feel is right. Throughout our life, we have been misinformed about things. We have had our pathways chosen for us, but it's about time we take control of ourselves. Before making vital decisions, it is essential to ask yourself, as you would ask a friend about what you want to do.

Chapter 2 revolved around being happy and feeling grateful. Perfection does not exist in life, so neither is it ideal to go expecting complete bliss in your marriage or relationships nor is it practical to be treated terribly and accepting those conditions. No matter what, make sure you are not compromising on your overall happiness and be grateful for the pleasant things.

Next, we discussed the importance of having good people close by who love us. It is so important to prioritise them, look after them and be there for them as they are there for us. Chapter 4 then taught us about the importance of not regretting. It is centred on making our decisions ourselves and taking accountability for them. Letting regret bring us down is like constantly valuing your past over your present.

The next chapter focused on not leaving the keys to our happiness with someone else. It is alright if the bond is organic, but nobody should feel as much as a window of opportunity to bring you down. Chapter 6 brought us face to face with the reality of life's unpleasantness. It is up to us to extract the goodness out of the bad things life offers. We are the ones who give meaning to our experiences and choose their influence on us.

Chapter 8 taught us that life has no simple answers. The right path will often be more difficult. Life does not come easy, but if we take it as a challenge and play along, we will find ourselves enjoying life like a game. In chapter 9, we learned about the importance of moving on. Crying over spilt milk, regretting, wallowing in the hurt of all that has happened will not serve us in the long run. We have goals to reach and dreams to fulfil. That can only be done by moving forward in life.

Finally, chapter 10 revised for us the importance of believing in ourselves. Opposing circumstances and the negative influence of people becomes easy when we change the way we look at things to serve our self-belief. We may not always find support for self-belief, but when we do, we should allow it to fuel us.

And with that, the fantastic journey of this book comes to an end, but it's not the end truly. It's a beautiful beginning of life...

Printed in Great Britain
by Amazon

80995548R00074